MOTHER
COUNTRY

MOTHER COUNTRY

*Real Stories
of the
Windrush Children*

Edited by

Charlie Brinkhurst-Cuff

HEADLINE

Copyright © 2018 Charlie Brinkhurst-Cuff

The right of Charlie Brinkhurst-Cuff to be identified as the Author of
the Work has been asserted by her in accordance with the
Copyright, Designs and Patents Act 1988.

First published in Great Britain in 2018
by HEADLINE PUBLISHING GROUP

1

Apart from any use permitted under UK copyright law, this publication may
only be reproduced, stored, or transmitted, in any form, or by any means,
with prior permission in writing of the publishers or, in the case of
reprographic production, in accordance with the terms of licences
issued by the Copyright Licensing Agency.

Extract from 'The Death of Joy Gardner', *Propa Propaganda* © 1996 Benjamin Zephaniah,
reprinted by permission of Bloodaxe Books.

Every effort has been made to fulfil requirements with regard to
reproducing copyright material. The author and publisher will be glad
to rectify any omissions at the earliest opportunity.

Cataloguing in Publication Data is available from the British Library

Hardback ISBN 978 1 4722 6190 8

Hachette is not responsible for the contents of third party websites

Typeset in Garamond by CC Book Production
Printed and bound in Great Britain by CPI Group (UK) Ltd, Croydon CR0 4YY

Headline's policy is to use papers that are natural, renewable and
recyclable products and made from wood grown in sustainable forests.
The logging and manufacturing processes are expected to conform
to the environmental regulations of the country of origin.

HEADLINE PUBLISHING GROUP
An Hachette UK Company
Carmelite House
50 Victoria Embankment
London
EC4Y 0DZ

www.headline.co.uk
www.hachette.co.uk

To my Nanny Teneta and the grandfather I never met, George (Fernando). Brave enough to take to the seas and bold enough to stay.

Contents

Contents

FOREWORD

David Lammy

David Lammy MP was born in Tottenham in 1972, one of five children raised by a single mother. He became the first black Briton to study a Masters in Law at Harvard Law School, graduating in 1997. Since 2000, David has been the Labour Member of Parliament for his home constituency of Tottenham. In Parliament, he led the campaign for Windrush British citizens, forcing the Home Secretary to guarantee the citizenship of Commonwealth nationals, set up a specialist Commonwealth Taskforce and establish a compensation scheme.

When my father left Guyana for Britain in 1956, at the age of twenty-four, he was young, athletic and cocky. He was well educated, thanks to his father's hard work in rice, cane and coconut farming, and had developed an urge to discover new parts of the world. Through an Assisted Passage Scheme, he had the opportunity to immigrate to the UK and become a taxidermist. He hoped the move would eventually allow him to move into his desired vocation, pharmacy, in new surroundings, and perhaps with more wealth.

It was with this vision in mind that he joined twelve other men on an old Dakota DC-3 warplane to Trinidad, before boarding the steamship SS *Luciana*. The great boat began its voyage by scooping up hundreds of other dreamy adventurers from the neighbouring Caribbean islands, before setting sail to Europe. On the six-week voyage, my father's easy worldliness – cultivated on previous trips across the Americas – was tested. His lofty ambitions to build a new life, with a new career, in a new country were confronted by the gruelling reality of mid-twentieth century, long-distance boat travel. Indeed, one of my father's travelling companions later told me that he had spent much of the trip below deck, enjoying face-time with the latrine.

Arriving at the port in Genoa, he and his band of compatriots must have been overwhelmed by the new smells, white faces and European accents. But they did not stay long in Italy. The next stage of their journey was by train across Europe. Zigzagging their way through France, they finally reached Southampton by ferry. There, of course, it was raining, grey and, quite literally, a world apart from the sweltering heat of Guyana. The band of brothers moved fast from Southampton to a cramped doss-house in Stoke Newington. Just like this, their new life had begun.

The tale of my father's journey to the UK is very different to my mother's, who arrived by plane to Gatwick in 1970. Hers is in turn different to those of my aunts and uncles, and different again from the many other stories you will read about in this volume. Each narrative is unique, but paradoxically typical of the hundreds of thousands who arrived in the UK following the British Nationality Act of 1948, which made citizens of the Commonwealth citizens of the United Kingdom, until 1973, when the new Immigration Act ended this right. Each and every member of the Windrush generation showed enormous courage, in leaving their home, family and friends in search of a better life. Each and every one started out with almost no money to their name, but with the ambition and energy to work hard. And each and every one faced down barriers, structural and legal, that limited their ability to flourish in their adopted country.

So many became public servants, in the truest sense of the word, arriving in Britain at a time of need. The post-war Labour government had a dream of healthcare for all, but no way of making it happen, and hopes for functioning trains and buses, but not enough people to drive them. With the workforce dramatically reduced by the injustice of war, the government could not fill the shortfall of nurses in the NHS or staff in the transport network. In my constituency of Tottenham, the hospital management board ran a widespread campaign to recruit British nurses in the early 1950s. It received seventeen applications for 737 job vacancies and just one qualified nurse came forward.

The NHS was desperate for a workforce, and found one in the Caribbean. The thousands of nurses and health workers that came to Britain before 1973 formed the backbone of the NHS. They worked with unparalleled pride and dignity – labouring for all of Britain's sick and injured. They were women like my aunts, who did seemingly unending shifts from morning to night without complaint, while caring for their young families. They were women who dedicated their lives to work in British hospitals, and yet struggled to be promoted from the more junior State Enrolled Nurses to higher-ranking State Registered Nurses because of the colour of their skin.

When we celebrate seventy years of Windrush, we celebrate the train drivers, cleaners and wardens in our stations, some of whom were recruited directly from Kingston and Bridgetown.

When no one else in Britain would, the Windrush generation did the low-grade and poorly paid jobs that kept Britain running. Seventy years on, we celebrate them. Workers like my mother, who did her own stint at the London Underground. I remember meeting her at Camden tube station as she would emerge into the daylight after a long shift. These jobs were not exciting, but they were vital parts of the functioning of our society, and brought with them steady, dependable wages. Nevertheless, in my mother's case, this salary was not always enough. When my father's career stalled, she had to make big sacrifices. At times she had two or three jobs, which meant working all hours. As well as her job on the London Underground, she worked as a home help, as a care assistant and, after returning to education later in life, she became a housing officer. She was one of thousands of heroic single mothers who, through gritted teeth and strong values, raised my generation to the best of their ability.

We also celebrate the accomplishments of those Windrush citizens who changed the shape of this country. A generation that brought us thinkers such as C. L. R. James, Stuart Hall and Paul Gilroy, without whom I would never have been a politician. Their words gave me an understanding of my identity in Britain that no one else could, and a political voice to so many throughout this country. A generation like Benjamin Zephaniah, Andrea Levy and Zadie Smith – who have given us all evocative imagery of what it means to live in Britain today. Windrush gave this country Frank Bruno and Jessica Ennis: proud representatives of our country on the world stage.

Despite many tales of success, the reality of moving to the UK did not always match the dream. I will never forget the first time I was harassed and groped by the police, after being suspected of a crime I did not commit. A lanky twelve-year-old, with big hair, a faded T-shirt and NHS prescription glasses, I was heading towards West Green road – a place that still feels, looks and smells like the West Indies. Fruit and veg shops, yams, mangoes, barbers and Afro-Caribbean hair products give it a special flavour. To get there, I had to walk down Lawrence Road, at the time an industrial area, lined with small, corrugated iron warehouses. Out of nowhere, three police officers pounced on me. One patted me down so aggressively, over my buttocks and balls, that I almost wet myself. They claimed that I matched the description of a mugger, but in reality it was because they could not tell one black man from another.

Even now, in the UK, we are eight times more likely to be targeted by the police than white people. Young black people in this country are proportionally more likely to be in prison than those in the US – and nine times more likely to be jailed than young white people. This structural disadvantage is a key part of the Windrush story, and it must not be overlooked. As a some-what nerdy choirboy growing up, many of those around me had more trouble with the police than I did. It was not rare for one of my brothers to suffer the indignity of arrest, or a night in the cells, for an alleged minor offence. One friend of my brothers, a boy named Reg, was beaten so badly overnight in the police cells that he had to have a testicle amputated the next day. Chinese whispers about these sorts of incident travelled fast on my road, and they only exacerbated our feelings of injustice.

Police brutality towards minorities throughout this period led to many premature deaths. One of the worst cases was that of Joy Gardner, a forty-year-old Jamaican migrant who died in 1993 following a disproportionate and cruel deportation attempt by British police officers, and whose mother is interviewed in this book. Police officers arrived unannounced at Ms Gardner's address in Crouch End in the early hours, with a 'body-belt', described by the *Independent* as 'a leather contraption for pinning the arms which has chains and handcuffs fitted'. The implications of English police officers arriving to physically restrain a Jamaican migrant, with what resembled slave manacles, are clear. The fact that the official post-mortem revealed that she died from hypoxia – the cutting of oxygen from the brain – is unforgivable. I vividly remember the incident being discussed on my street. It fit into a broader narrative of police injustice and 'us and them'. The incident echoed the tragic death of Cynthia Jarrett, aged forty-nine, during a police raid on her home in 1985, which had sparked violent riots in Tottenham.

Tragedies were commonplace among Windrush's second generation in Thatcher's Britain. Linton Kwesi Johnson evoked the anger and injustice of the 1981 New Cross house fire in south-east London, which left thirteen young black people, aged between fourteen and twenty-two, dead, in his poem 'New Crass Massakah', and more recently Jay Bernard won the Ted Hughes award with the performance 'Surge: Side A', a multimedia sequence which explores the fire. The establishment's refusal to prevent, or even to publicly mourn, such incidents created a resentment and distrust that lingers to this day.

But it is this year, 2018, which has revealed the grossest injustices towards the Windrush generation by the British state since Imperial times: stories of unlawful deportation, detention and discrimination that denied the dignity of citizens of this country. Ignorance of the roots of the Windrush generation, as well as the seventy years that they have dedicated to this country, is what led to the Home Office scandal this year. The Windrush generation has given so much, and asked for so little in return, and seventy years on the government thanked them for their service to this country by deporting so many and throwing others into illegal detention. Theresa May's 'hostile environment' judged them un-British, and declared that they belonged in countries that they hadn't seen in decades, if at all. They were told that their life stories were not British stories and that they did not belong.

Easter was a particularly gruelling period for London. On the bank holiday Monday, seventeen-year-old Tanesha Melbourne-Blake was gunned down outside a newsagents in the shadow of Tottenham Hotspur's football stadium. This sent the media into a frenzy because it coincided with reports that London's murder rate had temporarily overtaken even New York's. Despite being busy with the fallout from this spike in violent crime, I saw the Commonwealth Heads of Government Meeting planned for mid-April as a clear political opportunity to get the unfairness towards former Commonwealth citizens on the national agenda.

I was in close contact with Guy Hewitt, the Barbadian High Commissioner, who informed me that leaders were keen to raise the issue with Theresa May, as well as Amelia Gentleman, the tenacious *Guardian* journalist who had been reporting on the story for months. To create the maximum spectacle, I had asked my friend Lenny Henry to organise a letter signed by prominent first- and second-generation Commonwealth migrants, to present to the Prime Minister on the steps of Downing Street.

In the end, this was unnecessary. On the first day of the Commonwealth summit, I was granted an Urgent Question in Parliament. I arrived at the chamber early, watching the space fill up during Parliament's earlier business. I had planned how to use my two minutes' speaking time before entering the chamber. I wanted to start by speaking about my parents, both Windrush migrants from Guyana. However, as the time came closer, I started to be overwhelmed by emotion. I knew that if I started with my parents I would likely well up in tears, and fail to sufficiently cover the Home Office's failures. Instead, I began by rooting the story in slavery, which is where the Windrush story really begins.

Hundreds of years ago, late at night, 3.4 million of the Windrush generation's ancestors were stolen by British ships and taken across the Atlantic, to be sold as slaves. In 1625, Barbados became the first British settlement in the Caribbean, followed by Jamaica in 1655. These slaves were ruled over by the British owners until their emancipation in 1835, when much subjugation continued, as rich, white British planters dominated low-wage, black labourers.

Before that boat arrived in Tilbury in 1948, British colonisation had turned the Caribbean into a warehouse from which to extract profit. The century following emancipation from slavery was one marked by widespread unrest of labourers throughout the Caribbean, who protested their appalling treatment at the hands of the Imperial government. Ten years before the Windrush generation arrived in Britain, labourers in Barbados were earning the equivalent of around £3.50 a day. These extremely low wages left them and their families without food, in terrible conditions, and mostly without respite. In Jamaica, searing unemployment ravaged society, after Britain closed sugar plantations in favour of cheaper labour elsewhere. Labour riots were commonplace, as people became increasingly frustrated by the destitution that they faced.

The parallels between the hardships of those exploited by slavery and those who have been failed by the Home Office are obvious. Both sets of people faced injustice, in large part due to the colour of their skin. Both sets of people were treated as second-class citizens. And both sets of people were shut out from respected society, and forced underground to make a living. Following the scandal, I hosted a special Windrush surgery in Tottenham to help those of my constituents who had been affected. One of many to attend that day's surgery was Oliver Hutchinson. Made homeless, jobless, and denied the welfare to which he was entitled because of Home Office failures, he was in a desperate state. Living on the streets, he was forced to visit a witch doctor in Covent Garden rather than go to the NHS. Following the surgery, which the Prime Minister and the Home Secretary repeatedly told me would lead to no enforcement action, Oliver was arrested. He was taken to prison regarding a minor charge from two decades ago.

The story of Windrush must not be sterilised, or overly simplified. It is not only a story of successful integration, sport and cultural icons, or even everyday heroes like my mother, any more than it is only a story of Home Office failure, of systemic racism, or the consequences of slavery. The story of Windrush is, like any other, a story of humanity. Of life, love, struggle, hope, misery, success and failure. But it's one that is too often neglected in our media, which, I'm sad to say, is often whitewashed. This volume acts as a remedy to that failure of story-telling, which I ask you to both savour and share.

INTRODUCTION

Charlie Brinkhurst-Cuff

Charlie Brinkhurst-Cuff is an award-winning writer, editor and columnist of Jamaican-Cuban heritage who focuses on issues surrounding race, feminism, social justice and media. She is the deputy editor of gal-dem, *a magazine written and produced exclusively by women of colour and non-binary people of colour aiming to diversify the journalism landscape, and contributes to publications including the* Guardian, *the* i *newspaper and* Dazed.

For many years I felt I had been denied access to my Jamaican heritage. Flights to Jamaica aren't cheap, and Scotland, where I grew up, naturally has far more haggis than it does ackee and saltfish. But having visited the country twice now, I know who and what I am, which, it turns out, is a mess of contradictions. I have never felt more British than when I am in the Caribbean, but I have never quite felt at home here either. So the summer of 2018 will always be special to me. During it, I have woven through people's houses and minds, soundtracked to Jimmy Ruffin, dub and reggae, spiked by the high pitches of Janet Kay's lovers' rock. I have learned more than I could imagine about a peer group which has always fascinated me from a personal perspective as a third-generation Caribbean immigrant and as a journalist who recognises the mixture of sacrifice, curiosity and excitement that drew thousands of Caribbean people to the UK in the post-Second World War period, in the biggest wave of non-white immigration the UK had ever seen.

The United Kingdom was called the 'mother country' or the

'motherland' by its colonial subjects, but it was not maternal for most Caribbean migrants who touched down via planes or boats onto its shores in the period now known evocatively as Windrush. Motherhood in our society still represents nurture and love, but the UK was more a wicked stepmother of the Cinderella variety to those brave enough to make the journey: encouraging hard work and reverence of British society, all the while failing to extend protections to these new residents from the tarbrush of racism and later, the deportation orders served by the Home Office.

'Windrush' as a descriptor is inherently flawed. It was Susheila Nasta, the editor of a literary magazine called *Wasafiri*, who pointed out that that my favourite Scottish poet and author Jackie Kay once called the boat itself a 'fiction of a ship' in her short story 'Out of Hand'. Not only were aspects of the ship's arrival misreported at the time of its docking, such as the pervasive narrative that it only brought male Jamaican settlers to Tilbury, but it has also put a timestamp on an era that actually stretched back before 1948, and after 1973. The Caribbean and the UK have been intertwined for centuries, and, thanks to the tendrils of history, will stay so for years to come. The point made by Nasta was that Windrush is at its most powerful only when it acts as a catalyst to look both back and forward. As a connector rather than a beginning or an end.

Black slavery is the wider context of any book which lingers over the history of the Windrush generation, as it is the reason why people like my ancestors wound up bent-back toiling in the plantations owned by white men, already once removed from their real mother countries in Africa. That the UK was seen by the descendants of so many of these same people to be akin to their homeland, 400 years on from the beginning of the trade in the fifteenth century, is an abhorrent marker of the nature of subservience-inducing colonialism. Indian and Chinese indentured labour, a brutal practice which happened mainly in the period between 1845 and 1917, and put millions to work on plantations in the Caribbean, Africa and the South Pacific (in part to make up for the shortfall following the abolition of slavery) has also played a huge role in the Windrush narrative.

But while so many of our ancestors will remain voiceless, faceless and forever unremembered in the history books written by the same type of men who 'owned' them, I feel lucky now, as one of their descendants, to be able to help tell the future of their story.

All of the people who made it to Britain were pioneers, not only in their immigrant status but in the way they approached life when they got here, but this book arguably prioritises the voices of women: Caribbean matriarchs who held families together, tended to children and grandchildren and never stopped working to better themselves or to provide. Neil Kenlock, a Jamaican-born photographer who worked at the *West Indian World* newspaper and who is known for his 1960s and 1970s portraits of the British Black Panthers, lived with his grandparents in Port Antonio until 1963 (where he remembers sitting by the harbour and watching 'bananas being loaded on the ships to England'), saved his highest praise for his grandmother. 'She loved me to bits. She always protected me – if anyone said anything negative or bad about me she would physically fight them. She was a really great woman. A strong woman. The matriarch of our family.'

The renewed interest in the Windrush generation in 2018 has

come from two sources: the seventieth anniversary of the *Empire Windrush*, and the ongoing battle for justice in the aftermath of the Windrush scandal. Amelia Gentleman's reporting in the *Guardian* alongside strong work from the *Independent* and the *Voice*, revealed that the Conservative government's hostile environment policy led to swathes of Caribbeans who came to the UK being deported, or having their immigration status questioned. Even as far back as 2013, charities and legal advisers warned the Home Office of Caribbean-born UK residents who had been mistakenly classed as being in the country illegally. Before then, it was cases like that of Joy Gardner in 1993 (*see page 225*), a Jamaican woman who died during an attempted deportation, that broke the Caribbean community's heart.

Mark Brantley, the St Kitts and Nevis minister of foreign affairs who I met on the islands, and whose father was a part of the Windrush generation, said he became aware of a 'trickle' of people affected by the current scandal in 2016. 'Caribbean people have contributed to every facet of British life, and have been a part of the tapestry of the UK for a very long time,' he explained to me over a white table in the lobby of a large Marriott Hotel. 'We're all colonies, and that era was a time when our mother country called us. So it was particularly distressing to find that seventy years on, these same people that had responded to their country's call had been rejected.'

'Then imagine, too, the loss to our own development in the Caribbean, from such a mass migration of people,' he went on, a proud man who despite having studied at Oxford, never wanted to live permanently in the UK himself. 'These were young men and women, the people who were fit and in the prime of their youth.' The St Kitts and Nevis government were at the forefront of Caribbean nations who helped to secure an apology from Theresa May over the scandal. 'To use a cricket analogy, I think we prepared the wicket very well. By the time we came into town the weekend [that May apologised], foreign ministers and the prime ministers met an environment that was right for scoring runs.'

But even as the Windrush generation experience temporary sympathy in the problematic limelight of their 'good immigrant' status, other migrants in this country are still being cruelly, forcibly deported under the government's policies – a reminder that their fate as migrants can be transient. Shankea Stewart, who was sent to the UK from the Caribbean at twelve years old to live with her dad, has been denied leave to remain, couldn't take up offers at university or work, and missed her mother's funeral in Jamaica because the Home Office want to deport her. She is not covered by Amber Rudd's Windrush reforms because she is of the 'wrong' generation, and arrived in the UK in 2002.

'It affected my mind. I got depressed. I thought I was going to pursue my career, that I was going to be somebody. But then they said I couldn't. The Home Office don't care,' she told me over the phone. 'I got really low and I don't want to demonise myself, but I tried to kill myself various times. I couldn't cope. My mum was ill for seven years and I couldn't visit her either.' There are dozens of other migrants like Shankea who are, this very second, trapped in immigration detention centres like the infamous Yarl's Wood, thanks to our inhumane and cruel immigration system. As I wrote this introduction, my former journalism classmate May Bulman reported on the fact that the bereaved family of a

Windrush-generation citizen walked out of an inquest after a coroner ruled Home Office policy played no role in his death, even though he was suffering 'extreme stress' over immigration issues that saw him sacked from his job and denied benefits. But another story that she worked on was that of Kweku Adoboli, a Ghanian man jailed between 2012–2016 for the UK's biggest ever fraud. Adoboli, who has lived in the UK since he was a child, is being threatened with deportation to Ghana because he is not a British citizen, despite having lived in the UK for twenty-six years. His story doesn't fit the 'good immigrant' narrative, in two ways: his misbehaviour and his country of origin. However, it is essential to realise that countries like Ghana, Pakistan, Fiji and Malta are also part of the Windrush story (and are even encompassed under the government's Windrush Scheme alongside sixty-one other countries), as the colonial Commonwealth stretched far beyond the Caribbean. Ghana gained its independence from Britain in 1957, just five years before Jamaica. As put by immigration lawyer Jacqui Mckenzie, Adoboli's parents and grandparents "would have been born as British citizens".

Despite the trauma attached to many of their lives, it has been a pleasure to be able to talk in depth to so many people whose stories resonate beyond any scandal, or generation. Sharon Frazer-Carroll (*see page 105*) was able to recall the voice of her mother with astonishing clarity, a woman who worked her way out of living (literally) in a cane field to successfully bringing up a family in England. Riaz Phillips (*see page 241*) digs out a deep spoonful of Caribbean food culture in his exploration of how Caribbean migrants turned flour and water into bricks and mortar, while Corinne Bailey Rae (*see page 231*) ruminates on how her Caribbean-ness contributed to her feeling of being the perfect outsider in music (and why she used to dig the beans out of her rice and peas).

Like so many children of Windrush, I have found my Caribbean identity in small things, like knowing how to prepare and fry up tender green banana, and the surprisingly delicate scent of a rich-red Scotch bonnet. It's feeling the dancehall move through the rhythmic swell of my hips at my first ever grown-up Notting Hill Carnival; identifying the sweet, staccato Jamaican undertones of my mum and aunty's accents which mark them out to be children of Windrush, too; spending time with my Nanny, who I don't see very often; and taking time out to learn about the fate of the Tainos – Jamaica's original inhabitants, killed off by the colonisers. It's writing about race and trying to improve diversity in the media through platforms like *gal-dem*. Identity isn't important to everyone, but it's always been important to me.

While institutions like the Black Cultural Archives and the Windrush Foundation have been fighting the good fight for years in terms of platforming Caribbean immigration stories (now joined by new campaigns such as We Are All Windrush), charities like Praxis Projects, RMC Black Country and Birmingham and the Joint Council for the Welfare of Immigrants have been quietly working behind the scenes to support those affected by the scandal. Alongside proving that we can all take part by researching our personal histories and finding out a bit more about what has made us who we are, this book gives weight to the humanity behind the scandal – something that black people are so often denied. England is not our mother country, but we have found home here despite it.

WOMEN OF THE WINDRUSH GENERATION

Charlie Brinkhurst-Cuff

At present, as with so much of British history, women like my Nanny, who moved to the UK in 1960, heeding the call of Britain's post-war worker shortage, are absent from many key parts of an admittedly underexplored chronicle. As a society, we are only just beginning to explore how Caribbean people, many of whom made the historical transition from slaves to the colonial subjects of the sweep of tropical islands before the independence era of the twentieth century, have come to be in the UK.

While there have been documentaries, such as the BBC's eponymous *Windrush* television series, which marked the fiftieth anniversary of the boat's journey in 1998, many accounts seem to centre on the voices of men. The first segment of the series, 'Arrival', appears to exclusively feature male *Windrush* passengers. In Mike and Trevor Phillips's 1998 book, *Windrush: The Irresistible Rise of Multi-Racial Britain*, which accompanied the series, only eleven women appear in the biography of sixty-nine interviewees. In the famous, staged Pathé newsreel of the *Windrush* docking, the narrator claims that the '*Empire Windrush* brings to Britain 500 Jamaicans, many are ex-servicemen who know England'. The footage shows no women disembarking from the boat. On 21 June, the *Evening Standard* ran the headline, 'Welcome Home! The *Evening Standard* Greets the 400 Sons of Empire'.

Women's stories have been repeatedly forgotten throughout history. As Zing Tsjeng, the author of the *Forgotten Women* history series, once told me during a round table for *gal-dem*, 'Men do dominate history and the way we talk about it . . . People really struggle to name women's accomplishments and success in pretty much all fields.' Although in recent years, exhibitions such as *gal-dem*'s *Windrush Women* illustration series, which went on display at City Hall for the seventieth anniversary, the *British-Barbadian Nursing Revolution*, an exhibition and series of events at Guildhall, and the brilliant Summer 2018 *Windrush Women* issue from quarterly British literary magazine *Wasafiri* have highlighted women's Windrush stories, the male-dominated narrative around both the *Windrush* boat and the Windrush generation undoubtedly needs to be challenged in a sustained way. Its past presentation is a patriarchal insult to the hardworking women it blurs into its footnotes, and beyond that, is riddled with inaccuracies.

In reality, research has found that women actually went on to outnumber the men who emigrated to the UK from the Caribbean during the government-defined Windrush period.

'West Indian migration to Britain was characterised from the start by a high percentage of women; they even outnumbered men in a few years of the massive inflow,'* wrote Nancy Foner in a paper on West Indian migration. Margaret Byron, quoted in the same paper, has stated that Caribbean migration to Britain was 'the first labour movement in which women migrated in almost equal proportions to men'[†]. Gender and maritime historian Jo Stanley, has highlighted the fact that amongst the 492 on board, there were as many as sixty-five women settlers, from Trinidad, Jamaica and Bermuda, as well as sixty-seven women holidaymakers and 'colonial travellers' and sixty Polish women travelling from Mexico. 'I just got so irritated by some of the Windrush stuff because women had been coming over in the same numbers as they did on the *Windrush*, to do these jobs,' Stanley says to me. 'I was particularly annoyed that nobody had commented or had even noticed that the women, the lower-waged half of the population, were paying nearly twice as much of the fare and when they got here, they got crap wages because we were so – I mean we still are – so racist.'

The reason why women had to pay a higher fare on the *Windrush* was because it was a former troop ship. Either the journey was taken in an upper-deck cabin car, or down in the dormitory troop

---

* Foner, N. (2009). Gender and Migration: West Indians in Comparative Perspective. International Migration, 47(1), pp.3-29.
† Byron, Margaret. Caribbean Migration: Globalized Identities, ed. Mary Chamberlain, p230.

deck area, which wasn't regarded as suitable for ladies. While the men paid a cut-price fare of £28 and ten shillings (about £1000 in today's money), as advertised in Jamaican newspaper *The Daily Gleaner*, women paid almost double, at £43,* to be up top.

In her research, Stanley has also fished up the stories of individual women on that fateful ship. Trinidadian musician Mona Baptiste is possibly the most famous female *Windrush* passenger, captured forever in a black-and-white photograph, delightedly playing her saxophone to the men around her on board the ship, but Stanley has uncovered some details on the other women passengers, too. While she was reading the letters of travel writer Freya Stark, known for her books *The Valleys of the Assassins* and *The Southern Gates of Arabia*, Stanley realised that the 'rustbucket' she referred to was actually the *Windrush*. Stark had travelled under her husband's name so wasn't on the official passenger list.

Meanwhile, also onboard and sharing a cabin with Stark, was Nancy Cunard, a black rights activist and disinherited shipping heir. 'What an extraordinary thing that these two superstar footloose women were on this ship and nobody has really recognised it,' says Stanley.

Nancy claimed to have paid the fare of the hairdresser and

---

* Stanley, J. (2018). Women of Windrush: Britain's adventurous arrivals that history forgot. [online] newstatesman.com. Available at: https://www.newstatesman.com/politics/uk/2018/06/women-windrush-britain-s-adventurous-arrivals-history-forgot [Accessed 11 Sep. 2018].

war widow stowaway, Evelyn Wauchope, which contradicts other tales of servicemen pooling together to pay her fare. 'I don't know how much of that was about older upright men claiming "we were gallant, we did it" and how much it's racialised, really in that it's black people from the Caribbean saying, "We looked after her, not this feckless posh white heiress."'

There was a lot of misreporting of the stowaway, who seems to have become an almost mythic figure. 'The stowaway whom Claudette Williams and Wendy Webster name "Averilly Wauchope" is recorded in the log as "Evelyn Wauchape",' wrote Matthew Mead of the research previous academics and reporters had done on her. 'Furthermore, Fryer's article of 23 June names her "Evelyn Wauchbe".' Complicating matters further, a reporter for the *Evening Standard* interviewing the stowaway refers to her as Avril.'* But Stanley believes she has tracked down Wauchope. 'Her husband was American and he died as a medic on a ship in Italy,' she says. 'Then it looks like she came to the Caribbean and took up with the Wauchope family and married somebody.' After being in Britain for a few years, she emigrated to Canada, 'a real globetrotter'. 'I think she was a very adventurous person, obviously Britain didn't offer her enough,' says Stanley.

'Generally it's harder to find out what happened next in women than in men because so many women change their names,' she adds. 'So when I was using Ancestry it was certainly a strain,

---

* Mead, Matthew. Empire Windrush Cultural Memory and Archival Disturbance. MoveableType, Vol.3, 'From Memory to Event (2007). p.117

looking up all these women and thinking, "Where did she go? What happened next?"'

WOMEN BEFORE WINDRUSH

It feels important to acknowledge that there were black Caribbean people in the UK prior to the *Windrush* docking. Not only were there two other post-Second World War ships that brought Caribbean migrants, the *Ormonde* and the *Almanzora*, but women like Una Marson, who arrived in the UK in 1932 and became known as the producer of the BBC's *Caribbean Voices* and for her remarkable feminist and anti-racist activism, stepped on UK shores long before the MV *Monte Rosa* was renamed the HMT *Empire Windrush* and began its journey to the UK. Before her, there were women like British-Jamaican nurse and Crimean war hero Mary Seacole, who travelled to England in 1854.

Stephen Bourne, a self-taught and renowned historian from Peckham in south-east London, has worked tirelessly to bring to light the stories of black Brits prior to the *Windrush* setting sail, thanks to the influence of his aunt Esther Bruce, a mixed-race black woman born in the UK in 1912. 'I was sensible enough (as a young person) to understand that Aunt Esther couldn't have been the only black person in London during the Second World War,' he explains eagerly. Alongside writing a book called *Black Poppies: Black Community and the Great War*, exploring the vital contribution Britain's 10,000 black subjects made during the First World War, he spent many years interviewing Esther and eventually published her autobiography, *Aunt Esther's Story*, in 1991, just three years before she died in 1994. More recently, he has published a book called *War to Windrush*, exploring the lives of Britain's immigrant community through the experiences of black British women during the period spanning from the beginning of the Second World War to the arrival of the *Empire Windrush* in 1948.

Esther's father, Joseph, was a sailor from Guyana who settled in London in 1911. He married an Englishwoman, Edith, and had Esther. They moved to a working-class community in Fulham but Esther's mother died when Esther was only four, and Joseph raised her as a single father in the community. Bourne's great-grandmother, Hannah, was what he describes as a 'working-class matriarch, the mother figure'. This being before the NHS, Bourne says that these matriarchs would 'birth the babies for those who couldn't afford to have them in hospital and lay out the dead'. He adds, 'Esther was raised by her father in this community, so she knows my family, she knows Granny, they're all like one big family anyway.'

By 1941, Esther was a young woman in her twenties working in London. She had left school at fourteen, 'as all the working-class kids did in those days' and got a job as a seamstress for a woman in Chelsea. Sadly, her father became a casualty of the Blitz, knocked down by a taxi in Westminster when he was coming home from work during the blackout. This incident left Esther as an adult orphan, but Bourne's great-grandmother,

Hannah, who had known Esther practically since she was born, took her in.

'Esther said, "She was like a mother to me, she was an angel." That's what her actual words were,' says Bourne. Esther moved in with his family when his mother was around ten, and by the time Bourne was born in the late 1950s, she was firmly part of the clan. 'She had this broad Fulham, cockney-type accent,' he says. 'People would just assume, as she was an elderly black mixed-raced woman, she must be from the West Indies. They could not understand the concept of a black woman born in London, in 1912.' She lived a fascinating life, befriending Jamaican activist Marcus Garvey and making dresses for the American 'Stormy Weather' actress-singer Elisabeth Welch, before she passed, aged eighty-one.

STORIES IN A SUITCASE

In 2015, Catherine Ross (*see page 133*) and her daughter Lynda founded the National Caribbean Heritage Museum, in part to help document the Windrush generation's experiences before it was too late. Ross and her family moved to the UK from the island of St Kitts when she was seven years old in the 1950s, following their father who had settled in England a year beforehand to prepare for their arrival. One of the most interesting projects they've worked on so far is *Stories in a Suitcase*, an exhibition exploring what the Windrush generation brought with them to the UK. This included mock-ups of luggage brought by women and young girls, using 1950s–1970s charity shop items collected by Ross in the years beforehand.

'They'd pack their suitcases with their best outfits which would invariably be nylon or flimsy material and then it would be the wrong time of year,' she explains. 'It's an exaggeration to say they froze to death, but you know what I mean. They'd wear two lots of everything in order to keep warm. Some people came with as little as they could because they wanted to start afresh. Others came with things they intended to work with. As we're a very religious people, some brought things of religious significance like a Bible or a hymn book.'

In the exhibition, which has been on tour in different parts of the country, the suitcases show an assortment of essential Caribbean items: recipe books, boxes of 'Canadian Healing Oil' [used for pain relief], hairstyling products and lacy gloves. Ross says that for many Caribbean women, the natural path their careers took were as hairdressers, dressmakers, healthcare workers or on public transport. But, I wondered, why did the women want to come to the UK in the first place? Unlike many of the men who had visited the UK during the war before deciding to make the move, Caribbean women may have had less opportunity for travel. It is unlikely they would have ever left their respective islands before embarking on their voyage overseas.

'Most people were young – I don't think anybody was over thirty really – and they all came to work, for a change of career, or they came to study and further their career,' says Ross. 'In the main everybody was vibrant, energetic and was able to do three jobs – able to work long hours. The people who moved over were the cream of the crop.'

Islyn Wilks, a former seamstress, agrees. 'There were no jobs in Jamaica when I left in 1958,' she says in conversation with her granddaughter, journalist Ella Wilks-Harper. 'There were more dogs than bones. You went to England if you had a bit of ambition and you wanted to better yourself. You wanted to get a bit of cream.' She told herself that if she got a good job and earned a good amount of money, she could go home and buy her own property. 'The street was supposed to be paved with gold. But one thing it had in its favour, every shop window had jobs advertised and there were plenty of jobs. Plenty.'

Like many other Caribbean people, she viewed herself as entirely British. 'You had a British passport because you were born British in a British country,' she says. 'When I was seven years old I learned to write a letter and to put at the back of the letter on the envelope my address: Return to Miss Sang, Post Office, Buff Bay, Portland, British West Indies. And it was very important to put, *British* West Indies. Our currency then was pounds, shilling and pence – we didn't have any Jamaican currency.

'Queen Victoria. That's our mother. That's what we knew. That was the head of our little country.'

In terms of my own family's slightly less patriotic Windrush story, when I was last in Jamaica, my great aunty Girly, explained to me that my Nanny, Teneta, had left for England as a young woman, eighteen or nineteen perhaps, when she was in her late teens. She wasn't one of those on the *Windrush* boat, but she did travel to the UK less than twenty years later, in 1960. She lived with a bodybuilding uncle named Appy, before meeting my grandad and becoming a bus conductor.

Back in England, we had a conversation on the same topic for a *Guardian* feature* I was writing. My Nanny picked up a velveteen pink sack from her dresser and poured its contents onto the bed. Amongst old photographs and pamphlets from dead relatives' funerals, she found it – the British-Jamaican passport she used when she first moved to the UK. In the picture she looks happy and pretty, natural hair pinned back, small nose and wide mouth, wearing a spotted blouse and coin necklace. On her passport her date of birth is listed as 8 May 1941; Name: Teneta Morris; Profession: seamstress; Height: 5' 3.5; Eyes: dark brown; Hair: black. Unprepared for the weather, she was bundled into cardigans and given winter boots by the caring, tight-knit Caribbean community that was developing at the time: 'All the young people come over because of jobs,' she said.

'When I first got off the plane I thought the country was filled with factories,' my Nanny laughed. 'The smoke was high, high. But it was just chimneys.' After a long flight, she told me, she arrived at Birmingham airport on 5 October 1960. 'Three

---

* Brinkhurst-Cuff, C. (2018). Conversations with grandma: 'When are you going to get married?'. [online] The Guardian. Available at: https://www. theguardian.com/lifeandstyle/2016/nov/26/conversations-with-grandma-when-going-to-get-married [Accessed 11 Sep. 2018].

of us came from the district,' she said. 'I left my parents behind because they were too old to move, but I had four uncles here, and Uncle Appy said he was going to pick me up and I would stay with him. But when I came he wasn't there.'

'Were you scared?' I asked her, dwelling on how she wouldn't have been able to just call him on a mobile. 'I wasn't, because I was with the girls, but we didn't have phones those days like everybody has phones now,' she said. 'My friend's brother-in-law had to go up and tell my relatives where I was after we were dropped off in Wolverhampton with him. I'll never forget his kindness in letting me stay the night. It turned out my uncle had been in hospital, which is why he hadn't shown up.'

I find out from my Nanny that my Grandad George had two other children back home in the parish of Saint Elizabeth. He came over to the UK for work, and found a job on the buses. When the children were still young, my Nanny decided to join him, applying to work as a bus conductor. 'I dashed out to sit the test while he was at work, and when he came back I said to him "I've got a job, you know," and he asked me, "What are you going to do with the children?" I told him, "They're not mine, they're yours,"' she laughed.

Joyce Fletcher left for England from Jamaica in April of 1961 aged nineteen, a year after my Nanny. A tall, slim woman with an eye for style and 'dripping in sophistication' according to her granddaughter Heather Barrett, she didn't bring anything with her apart from a small suitcase filled with clothes.

'I left for a better life because that's what everyone was doing:

looking for a better life for themselves,' she says, 'Things weren't right in Jamaica. As a young girl I wanted to travel and people were going over to England so I went too. I travelled over with a friend's niece, but unfortunately my friend is not with us any more. He got elected to government and when he was celebrating that night in Jamaica he was poisoned.'

WORKING CLASSES

Historian Jo Stanley points out that Britain was in a dire economic situation at the time when most women were arriving at our shores. 'We hadn't really decided how we were going to organise our labour supply, and women, whatever their colour, came second in this process, because of the idea that men were breadwinners and women were not,' she says. After the Second World War, the country was forced to take a loan of $4.33bn (£2.2bn) from the US, putting it firmly in debt. Tens of thousands of British people had died in the war, leaving us desperately seeking labour from abroad. The government rolled out job advertisements in Caribbean media, and in 1959 the BBC Caribbean Service even published an encouraging book called *Going to Britain?* which had quirky instructions advising West Indians not to risk 'over-doing it' by working through tea breaks and hogging overtime.

'A lot of the women I have interviewed [from that period] were very straight ladies – really firm, churchgoing, very proper, who would've worn white gloves,' Stanley says. 'I think it would've been really quite hard to fit into that society which was just starting to think very slightly differently about what women could do and be like – be technical workers, not just nannies.'

Bourne, meanwhile, believes that working-class Windrush women simply continued the tradition of working hard and raising families. 'When my grandmother came back to London after the war, she lost her home. They wouldn't rehouse her and she had to live in the hospital because she was a ward cleaner. She actually lived in the hospital where Aunt Esther worked. Her children had to be sent to live with different members of the family. The war was a terrible time for everyone, and unfortunately a lot of the working-class people who had came from the West Indies had come into this situation.

'The streets weren't paved with gold, but they weren't paved with gold for the white working classes either. I think it needs to be put in that context. I can't see it any other way, because Aunt Esther was part of that mix.'

Lorna Holder, who came to the UK as a child and has had a successful career as a fashion designer and author, says that her Caribbean family never let anything get in the way of their working lives. 'My grandfather, Mr Alfestus Dennis, was an ex-policeman who became a Baptist church deacon. When he arrived here in 1956, he bought a very large house in Nottingham, and all of his children and grandchildren lived there. We were sheltered from all the rejection that many other Caribbean people endured, but somebody had to lay the foundation, which was my grandfather at the time.'

Alfestus, a strict man, drilled into them that they had to go to university. 'They wanted me to go into nursing, to be a doctor or something, or a barrister. But I chose fashion,' Holder explains. Alfestus's idea was that through education his family could save up to buy properties of their own. 'It wasn't about having to rely on social housing, or on what the country had. You had to be self-sufficient.' Entering the white terraced house where she now lives, near Hampstead, it's clear that his words stayed with her. However, she says it was her mother who was the 'driving force' in helping the family.

'She was there, you know? Obviously we always had to make sure we all washed up and cleaned up and everything, it was a typical Caribbean home, but she was the mother, she was at home and I never knew what it was like to go home and not have an evening meal. There was always dinner cooked.'

Holder published a book in 2018 called *Style in My DNA*, which captures seventy years of different fashion trends within the British Caribbean community, but also reflects on her own family's history. 'I think it is so important that black parents now go back to those groundings and that basis. We had really good values in how we brought up our children in the Caribbean. Good timekeeping, being respectful, being confident in yourself, believing in yourself. That was all part of our make-up.'

For her family, she knew that the aim was to carve out a life-style that could only improve 'and never, ever making your colour be that barrier' to success. 'The problem I find in this country is the class system. It's not so much colour, you know, because if you look at the white working class, they're just as ostracised. They're socially excluded, all the way down. So because of that, I've never ever dialled that much on the colour; I'm not saying it doesn't exist, of course it does. But I always go back to what my grandmother says: "Wherever you live in the world, there is always rejection." Although there is limited sociological use of the term 'white working class', Lorna's sentiment is reflective of many of the Windrush generation who are reluctant to place their struggles above those of any others.

'Many people felt when they came here that what they were sold wasn't exactly what they were told about. It wasn't the land of milk and honey, the streets weren't paved with gold, you had to work. But we found a way in Nottingham, in our little community,' says Lorna.

NURSING THE COUNTRY

Joyce's granddaughter Heather tells me that like many Caribbean women, Joyce became a nurse when she moved to the UK, and as a second-generation immigrant like myself, her upbringing around her grandmother sounds familiar. 'When I was really young, her thick Jamaican accent would sometimes baffle me and I would nod my head in the hope that, yes, she had just offered me another dumpling. Then years later I remember singing songs to her that I learned from a book of Caribbean nursery rhymes so that I could show off how good my Jamaican accent was getting,' says Heather.

'I also remember playing with stethoscopes she had hanging on the walls that she acquired while being a nurse in Lewisham.'

The government invited many Caribbean women to the UK to work as nurses as the need for health workers was significantly increased by the creation of the National Health Service in 1948, which officially launched less than two weeks after the arrival of the *Windrush* on 5 July. In a Heritage Lottery-funded project to collect the stories of retired Caribbean nurses from 1949 to the present which exhibited at Hackney Museum in 2015 in collaboration with Black Women in the Arts, their contribution to the fabric of the NHS was made clear.

'We realised that many of those nurses, now in their seventies and eighties, who arrived in the 1940s and early 1950s, were on the next stage of their journey. They were dying, or leaving the world, as it were, without their stories being recorded,' says Beverley Davis, project manager of the exhibition. 'The main things that came across were their commitment to the profession, their willingness to learn new things and their bravery for actually arriving in a country that was so different to the countries they came from. It was very cold, the food was very different and the people that they met didn't necessarily respond to them in a positive way. Often the patients weren't very warm and welcoming.'

Many immigrant nurses say patients refused to be treated by them because of racial prejudices. The BBC documentary, *Black Nurses: The Women Who Saved the NHS*, platformed the stories of the thousands of Caribbean and African women who answered the call. Allyson Williams, an ex-midwife from Trinidad featured in the documentary, said that, 'No one prepared you for how the patients were going to treat you. They'd slap your hand away and say, "Don't touch me, your black is going to rub off on me."' Zena Edmund-Charles MBE, a former nurse, loved her career in the field of medicine but has written* about prejudiced patients. 'Some of these were even retired teachers yet they did not know better. I can remember being asked . . . why did I have to come here to do nursing?'

There are countless similar stories, not just of hostility from patients, but from other staff members, too. Stephen Bourne's Aunt Esther once told him about a young Jamaican nurse who had got a job at a hospital in Fulham. 'She befriended her, and this poor girl was in tears,' says Bourne. Esther asked the girl what was wrong, and she said that the matron gave her all the horrible jobs. 'Leave it with me, I'll wipe the floor with her,' Esther said, and she marched up to the hospital and told the matron that she couldn't treat the girl like that because she had come to the country to help. 'She always used the fact that she was born here, as a way to say, "Don't mess with me because I ain't from Jamaica, and you think you can get away with this but I know how it works and I'm not going to let you,"' Bourne adds.

Strangely, one of the schemes to recruit Caribbean women to the UK as nurses was headed up by Enoch Powell, who was

---

* Edmund-Charles, Z. (2018). Zena Edmund-Charles MBE. [online] QNI Heritage. Available at: https://qniheritage.org.uk/stories/zena-edmund-charles-mbe-nee-josephs/ [Accessed 11 Sep. 2018].

the Tory health minister between 1960 and 1963 and arguably in part responsible for the future racist treatment of black nurses. Five years after his stint as health minister, in 1968, he became known for his 'Rivers of Blood' speech, given at a Conservative Association meeting in the Midlands – an area which saw steady levels of immigration from the Caribbean, and the place where the majority of my family settled. In it, he described the imagined deterioration of race relations in the UK and the 'cloud no bigger than a man's hand, that can so rapidly overcast the sky', of immigrants that he believed were causing problems.

'As I look ahead, I am filled with foreboding; like the Roman, I seem to see the River Tiber foaming with much blood,' he said, and in one fell swoop helped to foster much of the racism and anti-immigration sentiment that had been brewing in the years since the Windrush generation first came to the country.

'I guess it's ironic really,' says Davis. 'In politics people do what's needed in the moment and then change their ideas or their thoughts along the line. If you speak to young people now they don't know who Enoch Powell is, but when he was alive, with some of the things that came from his mouth you would not have believed he was one of the main ministers responsible for that recruitment. At the time Britain needed a cheap labour force.'

ENOCH, ENOCH, ENOCH

Although Joyce says that she didn't face any racism when she moved to the UK – 'I think I was too pretty,' she laughs – her granddaughter Heather believes the story is more complex. 'Although she stays relatively quiet about much of her past, I am wise enough to know that if she's avoiding answering something, it's probably because she doesn't want to talk about it,' she says. 'I am not about to add to the negative narrative of black women; I will not press her to expose her scars and struggles for the sake of my curiosity.'

Islyn Wilks also says that 'she didn't have any problem at all' in terms of racism, before revealing that her husband almost moved the family back to Jamaica because they struggled to find a place to rent and bring up their children. 'On the (renting) poster was always: No Irish, No dogs, No blacks,' she says. 'My husband Lenny said, "No, we can't bring up a child here. We have two choices, we are either finding somewhere out in the country or we go back home. But we can't live here."' They moved the family to Harrow, and became the first black family living in the area, a fact which made the local news.

She remembers going to christen one of her children and being disappointed with the way the minister treated her after they realised her black parentage. 'She was christened quite differently from the others. He didn't make the effort and I wasn't very pleased. I came out that church and right at the gate, I said, "That's the last time I put my foot across this door because my child isn't christened, she's a heathen." The girl beside me said, "No," but I said, "Do you see the way he christened her and the way he christened the child before? Completely different." In my book there's one God and there's one way of doing something – properly.'

For others of the Windrush generation the story is openly bleak. Race riots have punctuated UK history since the mid-twentieth century and, in 1958, commotion broke out in west London after a crowd of white men attacked a Swedish woman because she was married to a black Caribbean man, triggering the Notting Hill Riots. In the Bristol Bus Boycott of 1963, Bristol Omnibus Company refused to employ black or Asian bus crews. The 1964 slogan, 'If you want a nigger for a neighbour, vote Labour' used by a Conservative politician during an election in Birmingham, fostered more anti-immigrant sentiment. And while many of these incidents have been sparked by the death or mistreatment of black men, almost every Caribbean woman I speak to has witnessed overt racial prejudice and ignorance too.

Although she had a tough life, Bourne believes that 'by and large', his aunt escaped racism in her early years of life. 'It did touch her from time to time, but because she was living in a community, she managed to avoid a lot of those bad experiences.' One incident that stayed with her happened in 1931, when she was sacked for being 'coloured'. This was prior to the Race Relations Act, passed in 1965, meaning that there was no protection in law for employees being discriminated against on the grounds of race.

'She'd worked in a famous department store called Barkers of

Kensington in the linen room,' Bourne says. A new boss came in who kept staring at her, and eventually called her into the office and fired her because he 'didn't want coloured people' working in the store. 'So she went home, told her dad, her dad stormed up there the next day, had a go at him but couldn't get him to change his mind,' says Bourne. 'He went to the MP for Hammersmith and Fulham who didn't do anything. There was no protection.

'When she told me the story she broke down crying, and what she then went on to say was that "The people that I lived with in Fulham wouldn't treat me like that."'

Much like my Nanny, who remembers people chanting 'Enoch, Enoch, Enoch' on the buses and being afraid to go to the top deck to do her job in case she was attacked, Esther did see a change in how black people were treated in the UK after the Notting Hill Riots in 1958, and again in 1968 after 'Rivers of Blood'. But as a friendly, gregarious woman, she was hugely welcoming of the Windrush generation and would 'just naturally gravitate towards them, and talk to them if they needed advice or protection'.

Esther went through another horrible racist incident when her cousin visited from Guyana in 1959. He wanted to see a bit of England, and so they headed to Windsor Castle for a day out. The day soured after they tried to go for a drink in the pub and her cousin was denied service. 'She stormed up to the counter and said, "Why haven't you served my cousin?"' The pub claimed they were closed but she could see they were serving other people. 'She said, "How dare you, I'm British, we don't want your drink anyway" and just grabbed her cousin and walked out,' says Bourne.

Cheryl Pearce, who came to the UK from Barbados in 1964 when she was ten years old, says that, for her, it was at school where she first realised there were problems: 'I remember a teacher had put on display a piece of work which said that black people lived in treehouses or mud huts because we were monkeys. Luckily there was one black prefect in the school who marched to the head teacher's office to complain and get it taken down,' she says. 'I thought it was so stupid.'

Everine Shand, from Jamaica, moved to the UK at a similar age in 1972 and says she also remembers being called racist names at school: 'I didn't understand and thought the white kids were just being friendly,' she says. 'It was later when I made friends with the few black kids that were at the school I began to understand that these white kids were making derogatory remarks.'

When she had been at the school for a little while, Shand made friends with an English girl from her class named Sheree. But when she would go round to the girl's house before school, Sheree's mother wouldn't let her in: 'She looked at me with sadness in her eyes, and said, "Everine, I'm sorry but you can't come in." I didn't think much of it at the time, I just waited for Sheree and I continued to call for her each morning. I'd just knock and move away from the door. It became apparent years later that her dad was racist, and had instructed his wife never to invite me into their home. Sheree was also told to stop mixing with "the likes of us", but she flatly refused.' Not all of this racism was unique to women and girls but in some instances it was certainly exacerbated by their gender.

REUNIONS

Jamaica, as I discovered when I visited for the first time in 2016, is a lush, beautiful place. It's constantly hot, with crystalline clear waters, clean, white-sand dusted coastlines, flowers and mangoes, coconuts and big green breadfruit dripping from every tree. But its sandy beaches, winding rivers and plantation crops have soaked up a lot of blood and tears thanks to the tragic succession of events which could never have taken place if it wasn't for the cruelty of European white men who raped, pillaged and stole women and men from Africa and brought them to the Caribbean tropics to work, and later, indentured workers from Asia.

I often think of the second tragic journey these people were encouraged to take to the UK, but not so much of those they left behind. On a trip to Jamaica, my great aunty Girly tells me that she doesn't think she will see the rest of her family again before she dies. Sitting amongst pink scatter cushions, teddy bears and lacy throws in her pink-painted living room, she explains that out of almost a dozen siblings she was now the only one left alive in their homeland. The rest were scattered – some in America and Canada, but mainly in the mother country, the UK. Speaking about my Nanny, Teneta, she tells me that she longs to see her again. 'My heart hurts for her,' she says, 'I didn't really grow up with a sister.'

Academics such as Elaine Arnold have written explicitly about the psychological impact that Caribbean immigration has on families, and specifically upon mothers, suggesting it was perhaps a less brutal recreation of that initial trauma of separation that happened during the slave trade, when family members were sold off to different plantations. However, in general very little has been written about the existence of barrel children (*see page 217*), who, as described by journalist Kuba Shand-Baptiste (the daughter of interviewee Everine Shand) writing in the *Pool*,* 'were often left behind as their parents travelled overseas. Nor the experiences of the mothers themselves, who, out of necessity, had to make the decision to leave their children for foreign lands, sending gifts, food and money from Britain during their absence.'

'The experiences of immigration were traumatic for a large number of families, who were not helped to mourn the loss of their families and all that was familiar and dear to them,'† Arnold wrote in the introduction to her book, *Working with Families of African Caribbean Origin*. She went on to detail studies she conducted on 'the phenomenon of separation of African Caribbean mothers from their young children for long periods of time'.‡ The

---

* Shand Baptiste, K. (2018). My Mother Became A 'Barrel Child' Of 1960s Jamaica. This Is Her Story. [online] The-pool.com. Available at: https://www.the-pool.com/life/life-honestly/2017/43/kuba-shand-baptiste-on-mother-being-a-barrel-child-in-jamaica/kuba-shand-baptiste-on-mother-being-a-barrel-child-in-jamaica [Accessed 11 Sep. 2018].

† Arnold, Elaine. Working with Families of African Caribbean Origin (2011), p.13.

‡ Arnold, Elaine, p.15.

outcome of those studies suggest that of the Windrush generation, it was the mothers and children who particularly struggled
with 'traumatic reunions'.

'You know, Charlie, there was never a day around that time
where people weren't crying and waving goodbye to loved ones,'
Lorna Holder says to me about when her mother left her to go to
England. 'I always remember my great-grandma used to say, "There
goes another one, off to the motherland." Because people were just
packing up and leaving for a better life. And when my mother came
over and left me with my great-grandmother it was very sad.

'With the displacement, and people just waiting for letters,
and feeling isolated, you realised that migration isn't such a brilliant thing. It draws away the soul from a country.'

Holder took the plane to the UK with her young uncle Horace,
who was eighteen. 'We flew from Palisadoes Airport and stayed
overnight in New York, which was a fantastic experience,' she
says. 'When we arrived at Gatwick Airport my mother collected
us in the car. I was scared stiff, coming into this huge house with
baths, a garden, lots of fruit trees and so forth, and seeing aunts,
and relatives that I hadn't seen for many years. I didn't remember
my grandfather at all.'

When she went back to Jamaica for the first time, aged twenty-
three, she remembers that 'everything was smaller because I was
bigger', and was overcome with the sadness of the family breaking
up. She has thought a lot about 'the ones that are sort of left
behind, with just memories'. Which is why, she believes, 'it's so
important for people to acknowledge Windrush, acknowledge

the sacrifice, because it was a big sacrifice. Huge sacrifice. And then you sort of come here and you are probably struggling very hard, because what you've given up is that huge part of that heritage. You have that sense of longing for a family unit because yours is now dysfunctional.'

Arnold also wrote that in this time period, Caribbean women were 'frequently (living) as single parents'* in the UK. For reference, the Runnymede Trust states† that 59 per cent of black Caribbean and 61 per cent of children in mixed-race households grow up in single-parent families, with nine out of ten lone-parent families headed by a woman. The overall proportion of children in the UK living with a lone parent is much lower, at 22 per cent. It's not hard to equate this large proportion of single woman-led families to the creation of the archetypal Caribbean-British matriarch, who often presides over sprawling families with complex relationships.

Valerie Mcintosh, a bright-eyed grandmother living in Plumstead, is a classic example. Sitting at her house, I have the privilege of dunking her chewy, handmade roti into a chicken stew while she tells me about growing up in a little village in Guyana called Cumberland, in the county of Berbice. She had seven sisters and six brothers. 'We were a very very close family. There was a lot

---

* Arnold, Elaine, p.15.
† Runnymedetrust.org. (2018). Runnymede Trust / Fact Sheet. [online] Available at: https://www.runnymedetrust.org/projects-and-publications/parliament/past-participation-and-politics/david-lammy-on-fatherhood/fact-sheet.html [Accessed 11 Sep. 2018].

of yard space so we would just sit out and play. We mainly did everything for ourselves. We had a rice field, we had donkeys that we would ride sometimes. At Christmas time, when my father was alive, we would sit in the donkey cart to go to town to see the lights they would put up – hanging our feet off the back and dangling our legs and singing.'

Her father was a gold-digger (not in the Kanye West sense), who would go away to mine in different parts of the country, 'get my mother pregnant again' and go back to work. 'When she got fed up with him going away for so long he changed his job and worked at the sugar plantation,' Mcintosh explains. 'We had a happy childhood.' Her father was called Cyril, and her mother Queen Elizabeth. 'Queenie!' Mcintosh laughs radiantly at the memory.

She left the family nest after becoming a teacher and getting married in 1960. She came to the UK in 1961, on 5 January. 'I wouldn't forget [the date]. We came by boat and it took three weeks. I wasn't sick, but I felt nauseous. We came into Portsmouth, and from there we got the train to Waterloo.' She was shocked at the fact that in the first places they rented, they had to cook in the same, tiny-windowed room they ate in and slept in. 'Is this how people live? I thought. It really distressed me because we had twenty-three windows at our house back home and we never cooked in the same room.'

Her husband, Milton, who worked as a civil servant in Guyana, had come to the country to study law. They had met while Mcintosh was on a 'rebound' after she fell out with her boyfriend. She shows me a picture from an old photo album of him, looking smart and sharp-cheekboned, calling him a 'handsome devil'. Milton 'did his law, but he had an eye for the ladies,' Mcintosh says. 'Those days they were throwing themselves at him. And he had the gift of the gab as well.' They had twins, Monica and Michelle, a son Michael, and another daughter, Abigail, who sadly died at sixteen months of bowel cancer.

'He was brassy. He would bring the women to the house when I was in hospital, having my confinement for the delivery,' she says of Milton. 'Do you know how many beds I sold, thinking that would get rid of the sin? I thought that was the answer, I didn't know how to row and fight. I'm so silly, I would cry when he misbehaved.' Milton left the family home when the children were all four and under, leaving her to bring them up independently. 'I was very focused,' she says. 'I don't know a more sensible woman than myself. I made sure that they got everything [they needed]. I always kept a job.' She was thankful for having sensible children too, who didn't get into trouble while she was out supporting them.

'I never took him to court for child support . . . I thought to myself, I am going to bring them up and I'm going to bring them up well. I started fostering kids and doing all sorts to get money. I survived.' Milton got married two more times, and didn't ever reconnect with his children.

Her family now, including her granddaughter – my *gal-dem* colleague Liv Little – deeply admire the strength it took for her to persevere and provide for her family in a new country, without a husband and so many miles away from home. 'I am constantly in awe of my nan, and that despite the fact my grandad was a bit of a snake after he left her with children under the age of five, she was still able to work, raise them well and make sure that they were polite, respectful, in check, studied hard. As a single woman in a time where as a woman you would have been massively judged for not being in a relationship.'

Mcintosh went on to get a job at BT and was, Little says, 'really smart and strategic' when it came to caring for her family. 'I grew up with my grandma being the person who looked after me while my mum was at work and whatnot, so we've been pretty close from day one. I think I've got a lot of really strong women in my family.'

The journey across the seas from West Africa and Asia to the Caribbean and then to the UK certainly hasn't been an easy one. It has left scars on the women who bore the weight of racism and prejudice on their backs. As Claudia Jones (who founded the first major black newspaper in the UK, the *West Indian Gazette*) put it in a 1949 article called 'An End to the Neglect of the Problems of the Negro Woman!', 'From the days of the slave traders down to the present, the Negro woman has had the responsibility of caring for the needs of the family . . . of rearing children in an atmosphere of lynch terror, segregation and police brutality, and of fighting for an education for the children."* She was writing about women's responsibilities in America, but the sentiment resonates here, too.

---

* Guy-Sheftall, Beverly (ed.), *Words of Fire: An Anthology of African-American Feminist Thought*, The New Press, 1995

As a young black woman growing up in the UK today, there is a legacy to be proud of. Not only did women come over and have to endure difficult conditions, leaving behind young children, facing racism at work and betrayals of the heart at home, in some instances their history of struggle has been rudely erased. It is not hyperbole to say they faced up to their challenges bravely and unflinchingly. Inspired by Caribbean women who came before us, like Una Marson, later generations of Caribbean-descended women and non-binary people have also used their voices to stand up for black British rights. For those women in the Windrush generation who haven't yet had that opportunity, we must continue to tell their stories before it's too late.

A YORKSHIRE MAN
Howard Gardner

as told to Charlie Brinkhurst-Cuff

Howard Gardner is a retired engineer who lives with his family in Wakefield, Yorkshire. His father, Alford Gardner, is one of the few remaining passengers who arrived in the UK on the original HMT Empire Windrush *ship. At the time of the interview, Alford was ninety-two and living between the UK, America and Jamaica.*

There's a good reason why my dad wasn't captured on the famous Pathé newsreel disembarking from the *Empire Windrush* boat, which had brought him to his new life in England. Instead, he was figuring out how to get six of the dozen or so stowaways off the ship without being caught. He was one of the first people to come off the gangplank, but he got so far down and then claimed he'd forgotten something and had to go back. Instead, he went back onboard and gave his pass to the nearest stowaway.

He has memories of a stowaway woman, Evelyn Wauchope, also being on the ship. The passengers had a collection to pay for her fare, but my dad says that the chief collector was actually one of the stowaways himself, hiding in plain sight. At other times they had three men hiding in a toilet. The atmosphere on the boat was fantastic. He was travelling with my uncle Gladstone, and they'd gamble, play cards, dice and dominoes. There would be music all the time, because the Trinidadian calypso artists Lord Kitchener and Lord Beginner could make a jingle out of anything. The sound of the hum of the engines, or some-body tapping their boot against the deck. Kitchener went on to record at Abbey Road studios in the early 1950s, writing songs about falling down the London escalators, racial prejudice and, of course, cricket.

My dad was twenty-two years old when he boarded the ship in Kingston, Jamaica, and paid £28 for his fare. The only problem he encountered on the voyage was a 'no blacks' sign at a stop-off at Bermuda. He was born in Kingston, but his father, Egbert, who was a policeman and very strict, moved the family to a place called Springfield, in the St James parish. My grandmother, Lovinia, apparently looked after just about everybody in the area who became poorly and even though my grandad was a bit of a lad and had a few children by different women, if the kids by his other women got sick, they would be sent to be cared for by my grandmother. So she must have put her own feelings aside and been very warm-hearted.

Apart from that, all I know about my dad's childhood is that he didn't like studying history, and he couldn't see why he had to learn about long-dead kings and queens of England. Eventually, he joined the RAF during the Second World War as a teenager and was stationed in England from 1944 until 1947. He did his training as a motor mechanic at a place called Weeton, which was near Blackpool. But he tells me that he spent most of his time down in Moreton-in-Marsh down in Gloucestershire.

From there, he'd hitchhike to London every weekend to meet his brother Gladstone Gardner, who was in a different company, to gamble and see friends. A lot of people used to pick him up in Bentleys and Rolls-Royces from Gloucestershire because he was based in one of the more affluent areas. I would imagine there were a lot of questions for a black man with his thumb out on the side of the road in the forties, but he hasn't ever spoken about hostility. Most people knew why black men were in England because it was publicised. They were all passionate volunteers rather than being conscripted, and that's why they came back in 1948: to help to rebuild the country.

My father has told me stories of what it was like being an RAF airman back in those days. Having left Jamaica on the SS *Cuba*, he sailed to Guantanamo Bay and then on to Camp Patrick Henry at Newport News in Virginia, finally arriving in England, via Greenland, aboard the SS *Esperance Bay* on 3 June 1944. Rationing in the country was tight and he immediately got in trouble for putting too many lamb chops onto his plate. 'Airman, stand up. You have just stolen two airmen's rations,' he was told by a beefy senior. Later, he nearly froze to death during rifle training, but all in all he had a good time in England, surrounded by friends who nicknamed him 'The Baron'.

He left England after spending six months as a civilian in Leeds after the war ended, dancing in the Mecca Ballroom and staying at Greenbanks Hostel in Horsforth. He was repatriated back to Jamaica on the *Almanzora* in December 1947, one of two ships before the *Windrush* that brought Caribbean migrants to the UK post war. The winter he left was one of the worst the UK had faced, but rather than being put off, my dad had only been back in Jamaica for a few months when he returned to the UK in June 1948. He had tried to get a job as a motor mechanic in Jamaica, but there were none. He always says he'd have returned anyway, no matter what.

His first thought when he got off the boat at the Tilbury docks was to come to Leeds as the RAF were asking him to rejoin. He had been told that he could get a promotion, but when he found out that he couldn't, he looked elsewhere for a job. He'd go down to the labour exchange every day, and the guy would say, 'Sorry, son, no work for you.'

Eventually, one man who was looking for somebody asked him what he did.

'I'm a motor mechanic,' he told him.

He said, 'Can you strip an engine?'

'Yes, course I can,' my dad replied. 'It's putting it back together which is the problem!'

And he gave him the job. He had to fight to be employed elsewhere and eventually settled at a company called International Harvesters, which made tractors, and was there until he retired.

WHAT BECOMES OF
THE BROKEN-HEARTED?

The other reason why my dad was so keen to return to the UK was because of the ladies. He actually met my mother before he went back at the Mecca dance hall, but he was seeing a couple of other women. When he was back in Jamaica, he received a letter from one of the other girls who said that my mother was madly in love with him. The girl who wrote the letter actually stepped aside and left Leeds for my mother.

When my dad returned, he and my mum got together, and she happily took him home to meet her parents. But when my grandfather came into the house, he turned and said, 'Get him out!' My dad got up and just left, and my mum went with him. When I was born, the first out of my parents' eight children, my grandfather didn't change his attitude to my dad, but he thought the world of me. He even took us on holiday.

When my grandfather was dying of cancer my brother and I walked over an hour from our house at Hyde Park in Leeds all the way to Bramley, to see him. Because he was so poorly and he'd lost a lot of weight, he said that he didn't want us to see him that way. We never got to say goodbye to him,. He and my dad never made up. I can't remember this, but my dad says that my grandad would come to our house and my dad would just ignore him. They wouldn't have anything to do with each other.

My parents always had their own house, because the West Indian community banded together to be able to afford to buy them. My mum actually became the only one in her family who had her own house as everyone else lived in council properties. It was a big, terraced house, and my parents had the large bedroom at the front, while the rest of us shared. It was comfortable, although there was no central heating. There was a typical West Indian front room which we weren't allowed into, with glass cupboards and finery. We mainly lived in the kitchen, where the TV and dining table were. Everybody was happy and we were well fed, well dressed and well looked after.

My mum didn't work as she had too many kids. Within twelve years, she had nine children, which I've worked out is nearly seven years spent pregnant. One of the children died at birth. As the oldest child, when my parents were out, I was in charge, even at the age of ten. I have a particularly close relationship with my youngest sibling, Paula, who was born in 1963, as I basically brought her up. When my mother died a few years ago, the two of us made all of the arrangements.

Unlike some families of Windrush, our upbringing was quite good. I've read a lot of horror stories over the years from people. I sailed through junior school, but as I got older, kids would start to pick on me because of my colour. We had a group of lads, led by one person, who were quite nasty. They didn't get physical with me, but there were a few really violent fights between a couple of them. We had a bit of name calling at times which I don't like to think or talk about, but it usually wasn't physical. People used to shout 'go home'. I would think, 'But I am going home, what are you talking about?' You used to get women, especially old women, who would come and touch your hair. They would ask, 'Oh is that perm, honey?' But I did feel British, and I never really thought of colour.

My three main friends at school were all people of colour. There was a guy who was West Indian, of Asian descent, who came over around 1964 and because he didn't know anybody he was put with me. Then an African guy that came over, then a Sikh.

There were not many West Indians, Africans or even Asians at that time. Most of the time it was only me because my siblings passed their eleven-plus and went to a grammar school. My teenage years were fantastic, though. I got in with a group of lads, and we're still friends today. I have never felt like an outsider.

After school, I did engineering for a good few years, until the eighties, and then engineering in Leeds went bust more or less, and I retrained as a typewriter and photocopier engineer. Around the same time, I met my wife. We were at Whitelock's Ale House in Leeds and my wife's friend shouted, 'Oh, it's Jimmy Ruffin!' [an African-American soul singer] and that's how it all started. At the time I had a big afro. She went out with a few of my friends first before settling on me. I was told one day that she fancied me and as we were coming out of this pub I said to her, 'I'll walk you to your bus stop.' It went from there, despite the age difference – she was sixteen and I was twenty.

We got engaged when she turned eighteen, but we couldn't tell her parents. They didn't know any black people. They'd never been in contact with us and they were prejudiced because of the papers. So we were engaged for three years before we decided to get married, in 1976. At that point, my wife went and told her mum, and, at first, they were against it because they were worried how my wife would be treated. But she just said to her, 'We'd love you to come to the wedding, but if you don't want to, that's up to you.' And then she and her dad just changed their minds and actually helped to organise it. History did not repeat itself.

A PART OF HISTORY

I've been to Jamaica myself just once, for a holiday on my fiftieth birthday in 2011. I really did love it and I want to go back again. I felt at home. When we got to the hotel, the receptionist sort of looked at me and said, 'You're Jamaican, aren't you?' After I told my dad where we were going, he said that the place just up the road from where we were staying was where my grandfather was born. It was nice that we could look and see exactly what the area was like.

A couple of years ago my dad went back, and he got mugged. He had a gold chain on and was just walking around and this guy tapped him on his shoulder, saying, 'Hey, grandad.' When he turned around, the man ripped it off him. He did think about chasing him, but he realised he might have a knife or friends around the corner, so he didn't bother. My dad's still very fit. He goes to bingo twice a day and times it so he has to run to catch the bus.

I describe myself as a Yorkshireman with a Jamaican father – which I'm proud to be. I take people as I find them and believe that there's good and evil in everybody. And, I've never ever seen colour. I'm proud to be of Caribbean extract because of the legacy that we brought to this country, and are still delivering to this country. And it's good to know that while my dad might not have liked learning about history, he's part of it. He always says that, if he had to do it all over again, 'I would do every damn thing just the same.'

THE MATRIARCH

Nellie Brown

as told to Charlie Brinkhurst-Cuff

Nellie Brown was born in Manchester, Jamaica in 1918 and moved to England in the 1960s. She tirelessly worked as the lone matriarch to bring up her family despite her husband passing away not long after her arrival. Aged 100 in 2018, she still lives in Britain and is one of the oldest surviving members of the Windrush generation.

Manchester is high up, near the famous Blue Mountains in Jamaica. It's chilly, and you can't grow mangoes up there, but you can grow coffee. The place we come from is so cold it was called Colyville. In the mornings it's dewy and fresh.

Growing up, I had six sisters and two brothers. We lived in a big house because there were so many of us, and we were very close. Every day when we'd come home from school, we'd sit around the dinner table and eat together.

My father, Wilford, was a clerk of the courts and my mother, Christiana, looked after us kids because he wouldn't allow her to work. My father was all right, but my mother was just so lovely. Sadly, she died when she was very young from cancer and so my eldest sister, Adeline, brought a lot of us up. I was at school when I found out she had passed. The teacher allowed us to go home early.

I met my husband in 1935 at a party before I moved to England. We were dancing together, and he said to me, 'Nellie, I love you and I'm going to marry you.' I just joked it off. 'Go 'head, you fool,' I said. But after that, we did fall in love and got married when I was twenty-nine.

My husband loved travelling and used to visit America. It was his idea to move to Britain but I heard it was cold, so I told him I wouldn't come. However, there's a saying in the West Indies: 'Whatever your husband do, you have to follow him.' So in February 1961, a year before Jamaican independence, I took a plane over on a British passport. It was a bad, bumpy journey and I still thank God we landed safely because the plane took two hours longer than it was supposed to.

It was also a damn hard time coming here because of the racism we suffered. Everybody wanted to go back to the Caribbean when they saw the conditions and how we were treated. We arrived in the dead of winter and struggled to find anywhere to live in London. Only Jewish people would rent rooms to us, and I remember an Englishman had a sign up saying, 'Sorry, no niggers, no blacks'. When it came to jobs, people would close the door in your face because of your colour.

After a while, they figured out that black people were good workers, and then everyone wanted us. The first job I had was hand-stitching coat linings at a factory. You had to open the coat wide on the table and cut every little thread, and tack the buttons on. It was very hard and I didn't like it at all. A couple of years later I got a job working at an old people's home in Hackney, which I much preferred. I loved the old people and the old people loved me.

Back then, Hackney was a dump. I lived in Stoke Newington but we used to go dance at the London Palladium in the West End. The Palladium used to be nice, even if the people were a bit rude. Nat King Cole used to be there and he used to be a very good performer, a real joker. We couldn't tell the people there that we were from Hackney as they would've beat us up and looked 'pon us like dirt. But Hackney has had a lot of change and now everybody wants to come here.

There was racism in Hackney. One Sunday in church, we were ordered to sit somewhere else, and at the shop where we used to go and buy our groceries they would push the black people aside in favour of the white people. We used to have to wait late to be served. But there was a nice gentleman there, called Sid. Sid used to take me 'a grocery store every night at 12 p.m. He was a lovely man.

I cooked the same food here as I did in Jamaica. We'd go to big stores and tell them what we had in our country, and they'd try their very best to source it. We would eat fish, beef and pork – and you know we Jamaicans love our ackee and salt fish. Because of us, white people got to love it too. In those days we couldn't get ackee in the tin, but people used to go to Jamaica and bring the fruit over.

I also brought beautiful clothes in a brilliant array of styles, colours and prints from Jamaica. All the dresses we made used to be so beautiful and I remember a big Jamaican wedding for a woman with six bridesmaids, wearing a dress with a long train. The cars stopped on the roads because people hadn't seen a wedding dress like that before. I was there in the crowd in Shoreditch, waving and waving.

The only thing that sullied the wedding was the white people saying, 'There goes the monkey.' They always called us monkeys. One day I was with my friend who was a cleaner at the post office and while we were there we met one of her employers. She told us excitedly that she'd just seen a big monkey, but she was actually referring to a black man. I said to her, 'He's not a monkey, he's a man, just like your husband.' But some white people saw all of us as animals.

JUMPING FOR JOY

By the time I left Jamaica, my husband and I already had four children, aged between four and eight. They stayed there with one of my sisters for a few years while we were making headway and looking for somewhere for the family to be at. It was hard to leave them but I didn't feel like I had a choice.

My dear sister, bless her soul, grew them up nicely and they never felt unloved. She couldn't have children herself and she adored them. It was so very good to see them again when they came. I used to send my sister money and gifts for them, and she used to send me pictures – but I didn't actually recognise them when I first saw them because they had grown so big.

They didn't recognise me either. 'I recognised my dad,' my daughter Pam has told me. 'But you had put on weight coming to this country. I had remembered this very slim woman. But there you were. You were so excited to see us that you were jumping up and down, and when I looked into your eyes, I knew it was you.'

Not long after they joined us, my husband died in his fifties of heart failure and I think I know why. When he first came here, he struggled to get a job but an Irishman gave him employment, drilling on the roads. My theory is that the vibrations from the drill shook his heart, because he didn't know how to use it properly. He was just trying his best to bring home bread.

After he passed away I wanted to go home to Jamaica, but I couldn't because of the children, who had started school and were settled. Similarly to my father, I was left alone to bring up my kids. I had to run from work in the mornings at 8 a.m. to get them in the bath and off to school and come back in the daytime to see if they were all right, and then cook them dinner in the evenings.

It was a hard thing to get a black child in school. With my first boy, Tony, I had to make about ten trips before they would take him. His classmates wouldn't play with him either. When he got older, I worried about him being attacked by the sharp-styled Teddy boys in their long jackets and drainpipe jeans, who were quite vicious.

Besides working with old people, I used to work two other jobs to make ends meet – in the clothing factory, and then an evening job in the pharmaceutical company – and it did feel like a sacrifice. I had to give up a lot of things to look after them. I didn't enjoy life so much and I didn't ever have another partner because I didn't want to bring any problems into their lives.

But after they got big, things changed and they began to look after me and I enjoyed looking after my grandchildren. I would go back to Jamaica more often, and we built a house there.

There is no doubt we met hell here in this country, and the final part of my story is that of my grandson Robert Antonio.

He was stabbed to death when he was sixteen outside of his home, trying to prevent a fight. He was my favourite grandson, my baby. I had to be rock solid through the pain of his death to support the family. My daughters didn't think I would survive it, but I did. I'm very blessed with good health and I have never taken a day off sick from work.

Even at 100 years old, I am the matriarch.

MEMORIES OF A
CHINESE–JAMAICAN FATHER

Hannah Lowe

Hannah Lowe is a poet and memoirist. She has published two poetry collections – Chick *(2013), which won the Institute of English Michael Murphy Prize,* Chan *(2016), and a family memoir,* Long Time, No See *(2015) based on the life of her father. She teaches Creative Writing at Brunel University, and lives with her partner and son in London.*

I only ever caught a glimpse of my father's dexterity with playing cards on the rare occasion when he would offer me and my cousins a card trick. We'd gather around him in his armchair, a roll-up hanging from his lips, and he'd tell one of us to choose a card, memorise it then slip it back into the pack. Whoever was charged with this task would manoeuvre their card very carefully, hiding it from everyone's eyes. Once the card was returned to the deck, my father would perform elaborate shuffles, throwing the cards from one hand to the other, fluttering them between his thumbs, inviting one of us to cut the deck, before more shuffling. Then, as casual as could be, he'd run his thumb along the pack, flip it open to the five of spades or jack of diamonds, and say innocently, '*Is this card yours?*' It always was. We'd be outraged, confused, full of disbelief, begging my father to tell us how he'd done it. But he'd always be tucked behind his newspaper by then, a column of smoke rising above the pages.

Other than these infrequent displays, cards, and, more to the point, what my father did with them, were a half-closeted affair. When he disappeared after dinner 'to see a man about a dog' – his favourite phrase – I knew he was going to play cards or dice, sometimes in the East End, sometimes 'up West' at the Victoria Casino in Edgware. Occasionally he'd go abroad, packing his holdall and disappearing for days. I have a memory watching him 'practise' cards at our home in Ilford, Essex. He'd deal them out beside him on the sofa, scoop them back up, shuffle and deal again, mouthing the numbers and suits to himself. Now I know he was 'counting cards' – memorising discarded cards – a practice often used in poker, but banned by most casinos.

Later, my mother – a white English teacher, twenty-three years his junior – told me of my dad's old saying: 'If you can't win it straight, win it crooked.' She herself discriminated between card counting, which she thought was clever (needing an agile memory and good maths) and my dad's other methods – loading dice, cutting and marking cards. Did I know he did this? Certainly, I'd seen the paraphernalia in our hall cupboard – a tiny guillotine, a dentist's drill, pots of ink – but only in adulthood have I fully understood what they were for, or understood that my father was a 'card-sharp' or 'card-mechanic'. And rather than being glamorous or glitzy, like the casinos of James Bond films, this work was unstable and dangerous. He usually returned from his night-trips at dawn, sleeping off the game until lunchtime. Sometimes, he'd arrive as we were getting ready for school, the smell of tiredness and cigarettes hanging from him. He'd drop his winnings onto the table then climb wearily upstairs to bed. Those piles of notes looked like a fortune but, as my mother has told me since, it was £100 here, £300 there. Enough for bills, a school trip, new tap shoes.

As a child, I wondered who else was sitting around these smoky, basement poker tables, as I imagined them. My only clues were the disembodied voices of men who would phone to ask for Chick, or Chin, or sometimes Chan – his gambling monikers. I'm not sure if they were opponents, organisers, or associates, the same men who sometimes made dice tables in our back garden; the same ones he'd acquire 'swag' from, sometimes bringing home a few dresses, some jewellery or a microwave.

Looking back, I see that his lifestyle also enabled him to be a kind of house-husband – home during the day, picking my brother and me up from school in the afternoon, cooking dinner for us all when my mum came home from work. When he wasn't gambling, or cooking, he was driving – ferrying me to ballet, netball, piano lessons. I spent hours sitting beside him in the car, and it saddens me to remember how little we talked, letting the radio fill the silence. I felt shame about him back then – a complex shame, rooted in the fact of our racial difference. He was black; I looked white. He was also much older than the other kids' dads, who were milkmen or bank managers or, typically in our area, workers at the Ford car plant. How could I explain my dad's occupation, which I didn't even understand myself? In the end, I settled on the ambiguous 'night-worker'.

As a teenager, my feelings about him, and myself, shifted, slowly and subtly. I'd gone to a multicultural primary school, which I'd loved, but my secondary school was further into Essex, where Essex becomes whiter. There were only a few black pupils, and the curriculum was formal and traditional, where my primary school had celebrated difference. Casual racism was common. Someone found out my dad was black, and for a while, I was called 'white wog'. A friend's mother banned her daughter from coming to our house, because my father was 'foreign.' In history class, Mr Marsden asked us to write about an interesting member of our family. I wrote what I knew about my father's upbringing in Jamaica, using a word he himself used – *anglocentric* – to describe his schooling. When my essay was returned, *anglocentric* was circled in red, and 'No Such Word' written in the margin. I was starting to understand that those in the centre didn't need the language to describe their privilege.

I wish I had that essay now, to see what I did know back then about my father's earlier life, because I can't remember him telling me much. I knew he came from a place called Yallahs on the south-east coast of Jamaica, and was raised by a Chinese father, Lowe Shu-On. His mother was a black Jamaican woman – Hermione. The Caribbean and China were both present in our house through Jamaican sculptures and Chinese crockery, and, in their strongest manifestation, my father's cooking. He made elaborate Chinese meals – chai sui or roast belly pork – and Jamaican staples – stewed chicken, rice and peas. While my classmates went home to fish fingers and chips, the kitchen cupboards in our house held hoi sin sauce, jars of black beans, pig's trotters, sugar cane and plantain.

When I was sixteen, my father had a heart attack at a card game, an event that marked the start of a decline, physically and mentally. Home from college, I'd find him sitting on the sofa, staring into space. Sometimes I heard him talking to himself in the bathroom, asking over and over, *'What am I going to do?'* The phone rang less; he was out less often. I had a part-time job by then, and he'd sometimes ask me for a tenner to play in the local kalooki game. He was on blood-pressure tablets, and still smoking, making roll-ups from dog-ends if he didn't have the money for tobacco.

I went to university and, away from home for the first time, found myself moving towards my father's story, choosing modules in postcolonial and black literature, and later enrolling in an MA in Refugee Studies. My father wasn't technically a refugee, but the course involved the study of the push and pull factors of all types of migration. But I still couldn't have articulated the link between my feelings about myself and my father, and my academic pursuits. I still hadn't asked him about his life. And then, without much warning, he died.

At his funeral, the men whose voices I knew from the phone came to pay their respects. One or two I recognised, the rest I'd never seen, including an old man who caught my hand at the wake, and told me emphatically that my father had been the best poker player in London. Perhaps it was a custom in the gambling world, to send themed garlands. They laid them on his coffin – a pair of red dice, the ace of hearts – and over the crematorium tannoy, his favourite Billie Holiday song played: 'I Can't Give You Anything But Love'.

THE NOTEBOOK

When he wasn't playing poker or cooking or driving me around, my father was in the betting shop. He kept notebooks in which he'd write notes on horses' form. Those notebooks were always around the house. Imagine my surprise when, years after he died, my mother showed me one that, rather than containing racing odds, held thirty or so pages of my father's autobiography, detailing his early years growing up in Jamaica – more information about his life than I'd ever heard directly from him. It cemented and expanded on the hazy details I already knew. Here are the opening lines:

> I do not know the exact date or year of my father's arrival in Jamaica but my guess is about 1918 or 1920. From the little information I had of his past life he was born somewhere in Canton in China ... This vagueness comes about because my father, even though he had parental responsibility for my upbringing, hardly ever spoke to me other than to give a command in relation to the running of the shop which was his livelihood.

The notebook is a testament to all kinds of experience – a life under British colonialism, a rural childhood in Yallahs, an account of Chinese-Jamaican lives. It is also a sad account of parental neglect, detailing the dramatic changes to Lowe Shu-On's fortune, usually because of losses at Mah-jong, which brought about numerous relocations and shops burnt to the ground for false insurance claims. Various lovers and wives appear, temporary stepmothers to my father; siblings he doesn't know who arrive without warning and take his father's favour for a while. Most heartbreaking is the restrained way he records his father's violence – 'the most severe beatings imaginable for the most trivial reasons'. But it is also clear that my father liked to serve customers in his father's 'Chiney shop', as these community grocery stores were called, and which sold everything from rice to beeswax to plimsolls. I remember him talking of the towering shelves he would have to climb to reach the goods, and of the Syrian and Lebanese merchants who came to the shop to sell their wares.

Aged seventeen, he left Jamaica, travelling to America as a farm labourer, as did thousands of others, filling the wartime labour shortage. On return, the Caribbean had suffered a serious economic downturn and offered little opportunities. Of this time, he writes:

My thoughts turned to immigration as a way out of my predicament. I had been hearing from people that it was easy to get to England, so I started to make inquiries . . . I soon found out that you could book a passage on ships bringing back servicemen who had fought in the Second World War. So I duly booked my passage on the SS *Ormonde* paying the princely sum of £28 to get to England.

Many others, returning from war years spent abroad, found themselves in the same 'predicament'. The war had enabled travel, broadening their sense of the world, and they wanted to travel again. Poverty was a push factor, and Britain, the Mother Country, perpetually lauded as the land of hope and glory, was a logical destination. But rather than being the naïve victims of migration, as this generation is often characterised, unaware of British racism, British rain and the tasteless British food, many had already lived in Britain, or America, where the racism was arguably worse. As David Dabydeen reminds us, 'Jamaicans have only ever travelled for work' because money could be made aboard, but rarely at home.* And for my father, there was little in the way of family life to stay for.

My research into his life always has a duality, placing his singular experience against the broader historical context of the times. As a child, I'd wondered if my Chinese grandfather had taken a wrong turn on his way from China to somewhere else, but finding the notebook prompted me to find out more about Chinese presence in the Caribbean, and to understand this as a legacy of Chinese indentureship.

---

* Dabydeen, David, Introduction. '*Kunapipi*', *Journal of Postcolonial Writing and Culture*,. 20.1, 1998, pp.: ii–iii.

When I travelled to Jamaica in 2013, the Chinese Benevolent Association, a community organisation, gave me a tour of the old Chinatown in Kingston, where Lowe Shu-On had played Mah-jong, and took me to find his grave at the huge, dilapidated Chinese cemetery in Kingston. It was a strange moment, to stand under the burning sun, the cemetery covered in bright pink bind-weed. Their expectation, that I would want to pay filial duty, knocked against my knowledge of my grandfather's abuse, and the 'long-lasting dislike' my father held for him, written of in his notebook. The Chinese in Jamaica are a close-knit, family-orien-tated community, proud of their history, and with strong written and oral memories of previous generations, so it was surprising that no one remembered my grandfather and his Chiney shops in Yallahs. Months after my trip, an email came from the CBA: one very old Chinese woman, now living in Canada, remembered Lowe Shu-On. She had lived close by, and remembered an old shopkeeper she called Uncle, and his son, Ralph (my father's real name), who went away to England.

PAPERWORK

The recent Windrush scandal and its coincidental timing with the seventieth anniversary of the Windrush arrival, has reinvig-orated an interest in this historical moment, and initiated the replaying of the Windrush narrative on multiple platforms. My father's story is both like and unlike the dominant Windrush story, diverging in several ways, beginning with the fact that he arrived *before* Windrush. Despite the common citing of Windrush as an originary moment in post-war Caribbean migration, two ships sailed before – the SS *Ormonde*, the ship he names in his notebook, which arrived in March 1947, closely followed by the SS *Almanzora* in December of the same year.

I found my father's name on the passenger list of the *Ormonde* at the National Archives. He is listed as a 'clerk', alongside carpenters, boxers, musicians – a hundred or so others making the journey. The recent admission by the Home Office that it has destroyed the landing cards of passengers from this period, makes this and other passenger lists crucially important, as evidence of people's arrival at a time when the gates were open to Commonwealth migrants, legally, if not in spirit.

His story also diverges because of the nature of his work and his ethnicity. The commemorative practices of Windrush tend to celebrate the lives of those who worked in factories or on the buses or in the NHS – and whose contributions to British life are held up as evidence of their rights to citizenship. But what about those, like my father, whose livelihoods were less orthodox and, for a long time, illegal? Were he alive, would his experiences be seen as less worthy, or his rights to citizenship more questionable? I wonder how he would have fared in the 'hostile environment' that has affected so many of the Windrush generation, a policy which demands that British citizens prove their right to live and work here, through presenting paperwork that many do not have available. When my father died, he left few belongings – his clothes, a razor, an empty cufflink box, a post office account book containing £13, a pack of cards, his notebooks. He had no bank account, no National Insurance card – no official paper trail at all.

The ethnic plurality of the Caribbean with its communities of Indians, Chinese, Lebanese, Jewish and Syrian settlers would inevitably have been present in its migrating population too, but rarely do we hear these stories. Maria del Pilar Kaladeen's work around Windrush considers how the experiences of woman, children and those of mixed or different ancestry like my father have historically been erased from the dominant Windrush narrative, promoting instead a narrative of young Afro-Caribbean men, 'invading' Britain – a racism perpetuated at both popular and institutional levels.[*]

In Britain, the mix of my father's racial heritage would not have saved him from xenophobia – he still looked 'other' – though like many of that generation, traumatised by their experiences, he never spoke of it. But neither was he passive. As a teenager in Jamaica, he had been heavily involved in the anti-colonial independence movement, and in Britain, he joined the Communist Party, sold the *Daily Worker* outside Hampstead tube, and later, became an active member of the Labour Party. He read newspapers cover to cover every day, and had a deep understanding of politics and systems – indeed of the very system he himself had been oppressed by.

---

[*] del Pilar Kaladeen, Maria, 'Windrushed', *Wasifiri*, Issue 94, Summer 2018

I started writing poetry – my 'paper work' – about him, some years after he died. Poetry is the perfect form for not-knowing – it works with mystery and absence, and what is imagined, rather than known – the white space around a poem is the space for possibility. I took the memories I had of his cooking and card-playing to write my first collection and gave it his nickname, *Chick*. I also wrote about one bigot he was certainly victim of – my nan, my mother's mother, who never accepted my father and actively articulated her prejudice against him, while living in uneasy proximity; for the first years of my childhood, she resided downstairs and us upstairs, in a house divided in more ways than one. Writing has helped me understand all the facets of identity and to make a claim to my mixedness. I prefer the term without the word 'race', since I'm not sure now how useful 'race' is, when it cannot adequately describe how people feel about themselves, nor be neatly equated with nationality or ethnicity. Before, I thought my father's blackness was like an appendage to my identity. Now I know it is a central part, a part I cherish, and I am glad to be able to put his life – one among many important, migrant lives – on paper.

CHARMING FOR ENGLAND

Lazare Sylvestre

as told to Charlie Brinkhurst-Cuff

Lazare Sylvestre is a former mechanic and amateur/professional boxer from St Lucia. His granddaughter, Tihara Smith, presented her collection inspired by her grandfather and the Windrush generation at the Graduate Fashion Week in 2018.

I was born in Vieux Fort on the island of St Lucia in 1939, to a shoemaker and a seamstress. I was the youngest of five children and I had a happy childhood, but when I was in school both of my parents passed away. I went to live with my two older sisters, who looked after me and I was quite independent in a way, even though I had to do as I was told.

When I was fifteen or sixteen I travelled to Ascension Island, a remote British territory in the South Atlantic Ocean, on a contract with the St Lucian government, and worked with the United States Air Force on communication. As soon as I arrived, they sent me to work with an electrician, one of the men running wires around the island. But when he felt my hands he said, 'Nah, you should be at school.' He thought they were too soft, but he couldn't send me back because it was too far away.

Instead, he gave me six plug heads and a long wire, and told me to put a current in each of them without cutting the wire. When he came back to check in on me and I had already finished clamping them, he was actually very kind – he asked how much I was getting paid. I said, 'I think I get thirty-seven cents an hour because I'm a teenager.' He said, 'Hell no! You working like any man, I'm going off to put a rise for you.' And he did.

I was sorry when I had to leave to go back to St Lucia.

INNA ENGLAND

It was my brother who arranged for me to come to the UK when I was nineteen. He got me a job over here and was waiting for me at the docks when I landed on a cold Friday night in October 1958. On Sunday, we jumped on the number 12 bus in London, and my brother took me to Seymour Place in the West End. I started my job, working in Boots Chemist Piccadilly Circus, on the Monday.

I had flown to Barbados from St Lucia and then travelled on a ship that I think was called the SS *Montserrat*, rather than the *Windrush*. I loved the journey. We went through various Caribbean islands and spent almost two weeks in Tenerife en route to England. It rained, but just for one or two days and the rest of the time we had great weather.

I spent a lot of money on the boat having a good time, socialising and making new friends from all over the world. I met people from places like Spain and Venezuela. To entertain myself I had my steel pan, so I formed a little group and we would play songs to other passengers.

When I first came here, the cold weather was a surprise compared to the tropics, but because I had family and I was so young, I was OK. I spent all my time going dancing at ballrooms like the London Astoria, the Lyceum and Hammersmith Palais de Danse. You would start dancing from 11 a.m., when the places used to open, and if you had nothing else doing, you would leave the dance hall around 11 p.m. at night.

In the nightclubs, jazz bands used to play. It was the era of the Joe Loss Orchestra and big band music and people would be whirling round the rooms. There would be dramatic revolving stages and people would be dressed up real nice. I had on my colourful West Indian clothes, in a likkle sharp suit and a likkle trilby hat. I used to like wearing Italian suits and shoes. They nicknamed me 'tailorman' because I was so well dressed.

I fitted right into England because I'm a likeable person. I would be at the bus stop and people used to approach me, because they thought I had a lovely smile. I am a charmer sometimes. People would beg me to live with them, and I was always telling them no. One lady I worked with wanted me to stay with her because she was worried my landlord wasn't treating me well, and her children were in Australia. She looked after me like a son, bringing me biscuits, tea, a little liquor. But because I liked to do my reggae music, I didn't want to start bringing people round to her house. I knew my lifestyle may not have suited the quiet environment she lived in with her husband and I didn't want to disrespect them by bringing music and friends to her home.

I had some rough times as well. Sometimes I would fight on the road with Teddy boys. I wouldn't say they were racist, but they did think we were taking their girls. Sometimes I would challenge them and say, 'Did you lose a woman, why you looking at her for? What you want, boy? You lose a woman? Is that your woman?' Most of the time it wasn't English boys who were fighting us, it was people from Malta. The Maltese used to hang about the West End. Some blokes didn't want to go out because of them, but that's where I went, so I had to know how to defend myself.

I married my wife, Holifay Bramwell, at Sacred Heart Church, down Camberwell New Road in 1976. We had four children and now I have six grandchildren. She was from Jamaica, Mandeville. I knew a lot about Jamaica from school days geography – how big the country was and how tall Blue Mountain is, plus the main products of every West Indian island.

I was always good with my hands, and I started boxing not long after I arrived. I became a mechanic, working at Moon's garage in the West End of London, Piccadilly. Somebody who I worked with at the garage saw my build and decided to take me to a boxing ring, in Acton Town. He went to Lillywhites and bought me my shorts and my vest. I ended up representing north-west London. Then I decided to box for the Brixton district, and from there, I represented Tower Hamlets in Germany, where I was presented with a little pin from the mayor of Offenbach. When I came back from boxing in Europe, I went to night school in Peckham whenever they had things to do concerning mechanics.

Over time, I lost touch with most of the friends I met on the boat over to the UK, but a few months later I did have a chance meeting with one passenger who went on to become a policeman. He came into Moon's garage where I worked and I serviced his car. As a tip, he didn't pay me in cash; instead, as he found out that I was a boxer, he gave me the boxing gloves that he used when he was in the Navy, stationed on a battleship on the Caribbean coast guard.

My boxing name was Dick Reeves. That came from when my friend and I used to go to the nightclubs. One day, when we went in, the bouncers said, 'Boy, if anything happens in the club the police will come and knock on your door, they'll have your name.' So my friend said, 'We'll have to go and get a name you can remember.' My friend called himself Sally James, and initially I gave myself the name, Dick Rivers. But then I watched the film *Loving You* starring Elvis Presley, where the name of the character was Deke Rivers. I thought people would figure I had taken the name from the film, so I changed it to Dick Reeves. Most people call me Dick to this day; they think I'm joking when I tell them my real name is Lazare.

MY LITTLE TIHARA

England wasn't bad, I survived, and now I have my little Tihara, my granddaughter who I spend a lot of time with. When she was young, she always liked to play with my hair and ask me a lot of questions. Now, she's made a whole fashion collection around my story.

Tihara came up with the idea for her fashion degree final collection after going to see the Stand Firm exhibition at the Tate Britain, which explored the art and politics of Caribbean migrants to the UK. She started asking the family for pictures and looking at the culture, crafts and embroidery of where I'm from.

Her collection includes a coat that's made from raffia, with colourful Caribbean symbols like the doctor bird, bananas and palm leaves embroidered onto it. She went to Peckham and Brixton and bought the type of tablecloths we used to have at home, and made the clothes straight from them, in the style of the clothes the immigrants in the pictures were wearing when they first came.

Raffia is a delicate material made from the palm tree. They get the strips of the leaves and they weave them together to make the fabric. But you can get it before it's woven, just the strips and use that as the thread to embroider, which is what Tihara did. She also made a bag which has 'You Called, We Came' embroidered onto it.

I do a little bit of tailoring as well, and I'll tell her about the different stitches which might come in handy if her sewing machine breaks – like half stitch and double over bend. Holifay helped her do the crocheting for the collection, and her maternal great-grand-mother Merlina (Holifay's mother) is one of the best seamstresses I have come across. You just have to tell her what you want and she will design a dress for you in no time. Tihara is actually named after her – her middle name is Merlena (a slightly different spelling). She's still alive, aged ninety, and she's from St Elizabeth in Jamaica. Unfortunately she's not very well, but my family spend a lot of time with her. Tihara's mum – my daughter Lorna – had her baptism dress and communion dress made by Merlina.

Tihara has merged the experiences of the Caribbean and those in Britain to make her work and she thinks that more people her age should start asking questions about where they come from and see the beauty and positivity of the Caribbean. I agree.

STRANGE LANDS

Naomi Oppenheim

as told to Charlie Brinkhurst-Cuff

Naomi Oppenheim is a PhD candidate at the British Library and University College London, who helped curate its seminal Windrush generation exhibition, Songs in a Strange Land. *Her paternal grandmother, Joyce Elisser Norris, is Lebanese Jamaican.*

I uncovered the fact that my great uncle had travelled to the UK on the HMS *Windrush* in 1948 with his wife from a tiny clipping in an old Jamaican newspaper.

The clipping was sent to me by one of my cousins in Portugal, and I read it on the 23 June, a day after the seventieth anniversary of the ship docking at Tilbury. There was a photograph of my great uncle and his kids, with a strapline that read: 'Herbert Zayne and his wife were on the *Windrush* with their two children.'

I had forgotten the existence of this particular great uncle because he was rarely spoken about in my family. The half-brother of my grandmother, Herbert was the result of my great-grandfather's extramarital affair. Born in Jamaica, his mother was a black woman from a rural area who was one of my great-grandad's employees. He didn't have the same advantages as the rest of the family but was brought into their home when he was a boy for some years as my great-grandmother wanted to help him. Despite him being on the *Windrush*, his wife was actually from Blackpool in England. I think they met during the war, and he must have then taken her back to Jamaica in the 1940s, where they had two children.

Following almost a year of work on an exhibition about the Windrush generation for the British Library, *Songs in a Strange Land*, it was very emotional to realise that I had a tangible link to this particular boat – which has become problematic in the way that it overshadows and misrepresents the real story of Britain's Caribbean migrants. Even Herbert's mixed-race family's story complicates the narrative of the *Windrush* ship being filled with single men from Jamaica. In reality, the ship brought men, women and children from across the Caribbean. It first stopped at Trinidad then Jamaica, Tampico, Havana and Bermuda – disrupting the myth of Jamaican centricity.

At this point, I don't think you can get rid of the phrase 'the Windrush generation', because it has become a useful symbol that has opened up a discussion. I can see why people find it frustrating, but then, the post-war period is really important. It was different from what came before, thanks to the volume of people reaching our shores. Even so, we should acknowledge the fact that it undoes a lot of the hard work that activists, scholars and historians have been doing to move us beyond the 1948 moment. There were forgotten ships before the *Windrush*, like the SS *Ormonde* and the *Almanzora*. A Dominican historian called Edward Scobie wrote one of the first books to account for Britain's hidden Black history in 1972, called *Black Britannia: A History of Blacks in*

Britain and similarly, historian David Olusoga's recent book and TV programme, *Black and British*, showed black people have been in the UK for hundreds of years.

There's also the problem that since the Windrush scandal broke, some of the Windrush generation narratives are premised on the idea of them being 'good immigrants' – a patriotic people, who fought in the war, worked hard and loved queen and country. There are of course a lot of Caribbean people in the UK who do feel that way, but again that account of their identity clouds the stories of the pre-war black immigrants who operated against colonialism and imperialism, like Una Marson, C. L. R. James, George Padmore, Amy Ashwood Garvey (Marcus Garvey's first wife), Harold Moody and the later radicalism of the British Black Power movement in the 1970s.

I think that *Songs in a Strange Land* does a really good job in not just commemorating the Windrush generation, but also exploring British colonisation in the Caribbean, slavery and migration before Windrush, anti-colonial networks like the League of Coloured Peoples (founded in 1931), the mass rebellions between 1934 and 1938 that swept the Caribbean, and Marcus Garvey's famous speeches and writings that had such a profound and lasting impact on black politics and culture.

THE GOOD CHINA

I was introduced to Caribbean history thanks to an amazing teacher I had at Leeds University, Anyaa Anim-Addo, who taught us about things beyond abolition and William Wilberforce. We learned about the resistance within Caribbean slave communities and runaway slaves, and read their journals.

However, my first connection with the Windrush generation was through my grandmother, Joyce, because she always used to tell us stories of her experiences moving from Jamaica to England. Unfortunately, she now has Alzheimer's, and she sometimes has episodes where she doesn't understand why she's in England, even though she's been here for seventy years. As you forget things, it seems your identity becomes collapsed into smaller parts.

She moved over in 1948, the same year as her half-brother, when she was twenty. I haven't found the ship she travelled on, but I do know that her dad bought the ticket and that it was a nice journey. I think she travelled with a family friend *in loco parentis*, as they thought it was unsafe for women to travel alone. She came with two trunks of clothes, books and other belongings. One was a large wardrobe trunk with an internal top shelf, packed with beautiful hand-tailored garments and leather shoes. When she started working as a nurse people would steal her tights, but not her clothes as she was too skinny.

There's an assumption that people who migrate are very

poor, but this certainly wasn't the case for my grandmother who grew up in a privileged, middle-class household with her two sisters, Marion and Nabeeha, and her brother, Habeeb Fitz-Roy. In Jamaica, she went to the same girls' school as the governor's daughter, and passed her ordinary school certificate in seven subjects. She didn't complete her advanced levels as she had to manage the office of the family's tobacco business. She then worked in a bank before coming to England, wanting to move to get away from the confines of a controlling and restrictive family code that limited her ability to make her own decisions. I believe she had the sense of being in an empire and that there was this *other* place that she had a right to go and explore.

Her parents both stayed in Jamaica. They were from the parish of St Andrew, and growing up her father's tobacco business made them quite wealthy. All of her relatives were professional people such as doctors or music teachers, and they had a lot of servants. My great-grandfather, Habeeb Najeeb Zayne, was a Syrian migrant who had come to Jamaica in the early twentieth century; when she was seven they moved back to the Middle East for a year, which she talks about a lot. She remembers girls being married off at a young age, which is partly why her mum, Lily Elisser Machete, insisted they came back to Jamaica.

Lily was half Scottish and half black Jamaican. There had been some movement back and forth between Panama and Jamaica amongst my great- and great-great-grandmother's generations, due to the building of the Panama Canal when lots of Caribbeans went over to work. There was a family myth that my great-grandmother was the direct descendant of a black slave who had been born in the southern states of the USA and had a relationship with a red-headed Scottish manager, but I have no evidence of this.

Both my great-grandmother and my great aunt had mental health issues, such as schizophrenia, that were almost unspoken. Nabeeha (my great aunt) spent several years in a mental hospital in Glasgow, while Lily's mental health was sporadic, and declined with age. She was seen to have been 'dragged into' voodoo and Obeah and also ended up being institutionalised in Kingston. I think in the early to mid-twentieth century, you suffered from mental health issues in silence, or you had them so badly that you got shipped off to a psychiatric hospital. My granny points to her mother's mental health as one of the reasons that she left Jamaica, but despite this, it was my grandma that was the black sheep of the family. She was the naughty child with messy hair that couldn't be tamed, who had a stronger connection to the servants than to her parents. They would protect her from her parents and she'd give them extra food in return.

She had some backward ideas when it came to race and colourism because she was so light-skinned and grew up in a Jamaican society structured so heavily by colour. When I was younger she would sit me in between her legs, in front of the TV, cover my thick hair in olive oil and gently comb it out. My mum was rubbish with combing, but I think it was important to my grandma that my hair was as straight as it could be. She wore her hair neatly permed, and she'd put in rollers. Regardless, she's a fundamentally egalitarian person who was much more open and liberal minded than the context from which she came.

When she first arrived in the UK she moved to Portsmouth, where she met my grandad. He was a Wiltshire-born lad in the Navy and thought she was rather gorgeous. He called off another engagement so he could marry her in late 1949. A year afterwards, they had my dad William, and then my aunt Maria. They moved around a lot because of my grandad's job and she would often be left alone for as many as eight months at a time. Living in remote small English villages while my grandad was away, she didn't really have many friends or a sense of a Caribbean community. But even though her family was concerned about the match, because my grandfather came from a poor, rural and uneducated family, they had a long and happy relationship, especially as they got older. He was very supportive when she trained to be a teacher and would look after my dad and aunt while she was studying. They spent their retirement travelling, setting up home in Spain and caring for their grandchildren.

My grandparents would come and pick me and my sister, Maya, up from school once or twice a week, and sometimes in the summer, they'd stay with us. We would often go to Ridley Road market with my granny, where they sell lots of Caribbean and West African foods. She was an incredible cook and her food was a delicious amalgamation of Caribbean and Lebanese cuisines. She would cook us plantains, and roast sweet potatoes in the oven for when we'd come home from school. We'd scoop them straight out of the skins to eat piping hot. Her other dishes were stuffed aubergines and marrows, pilau-style saffron rice, rum-soaked Christmas cake and tasty stews. Walking through the market with her and eating her food was a root to my Caribbean-ness.

With her family and people she knows, my grandma is very loud, funny, giggly, pinch-your-bum cheeky and incredibly intelligent, but she is also very emotional. She'd always cry a lot, especially at hellos and goodbyes, and with people she doesn't know she becomes almost shy. My grandad died in Christmas 2017, and I think the Alzheimer's combined with grief is tough. She doesn't always remember that he has died, which is quite traumatic. Sometimes it feels best to not tell her the truth and let her live out her fantasy because she's going to forget again in a few minutes.

I found out a couple of years ago that she bought a china set named Oppenheim especially for when my mum's side of the family came over to visit, which broke my heart. Even though my grandmother on my mum's side was a German Jewish refugee who left Munich in 1934 after Hitler came into power, and my grandpa came from New Zealand and was in the navy, like her own husband, I think she saw them as being more English than she was. She felt that she needed to impress them, or at least not make them think less of her. This white and yellow crisscrossed set and all these teapots, teacups and plates are never ever used. I've eaten at her flat in Chelmsford hundreds of times and I've never seen it come out. To me, it shows a deep self-consciousness, a feeling of being different and not quite fitting in; the china set represented a kind of social armour.

I've never been to Jamaica and I'm really quite desperate to go. But my granny is like, 'Don't go, don't go, it's dangerous.' Lots of other people in the family also say this because they believe it to be incredibly different to the place that they left. My granny went back three times ultimately, but only after twenty years had passed.

Working on the exhibition has helped me to see the complexities of Windrush and to question the neat narratives about migration that we are fed by the mainstream media. It also allowed me to connect to my own Caribbean heritage, to pay tribute to this amazing community that my granny is unconventionally a part of. Gradually, I am filling in the gaps that my granny couldn't tell me about, realising the hardship that she faced as a post-war Caribbean migrant and gaining insight into the otherness she must have felt. I wish I had spoken to my granny so much more about her life; sadly this isn't an option any more and I feel deep regret for not writing or recording her experiences more fully. Seize the opportunity while you can, because our grandparents' stories are precious and the relationship between grandchild and grandparent is a unique bond which bridges past, present and future.

THE BLACK HOUSE

Gail Lewis

as told to Charlie Brinkhurst-Cuff

Gail Lewis is an academic in the Department of Psychosocial Studies at Birkbeck University who researches the intersection of gender and race in the formation of subjectivity and experience. She is also an activist who has worked with the Brixton Black Women's Group and co-founded the Organisation for Women of African and Asian Descent (OWAAD).

My mum and the man who is my father met not long after I was born. She was no longer welcome in her father's home after getting pregnant out of wedlock to a black man, and we ended up in a Salvation Army homeless hotel, via a mother and baby home where they tried to convince her to gave me up for adoption. Eventually, she was able to get a room at a big house in Kilburn and Roy, my father, also had a room in the house – which is how they met.

Everyone who lived at our house was black apart from my mum. It was a vibrant place of reception, with people arriving and moving in and out all the time. There were only three and a half storeys but all the rooms were let out by the landlord, and all the tenants were from the Caribbean. Music of different kinds would sound from each floor – jazz from ours, blues from our neighbours' Clarence and Pearl, and pious Ms May would play religious songs. It was owned by a Polish man called Mr Rakowski. Sometimes I would visit him at his posh house in Clapham, where they would invite us around for Sunday dinner.

It was a complicated place in terms of race. A teenager called Sheila lived up the road from us and used to look after me as a babysitter. Her white British family were fairly open and Sheila became quite close to my mum and dad. But in that very English way, things could quickly close down. If their families were visiting, they wouldn't let it be known that they were friends with us or anybody from our house. Situations could turn, and suddenly a racist comment like 'jungle bunny' or 'blackie', or 'wog' or 'sambo' would be made.

It's left its mark. In these Brexit times, I'm very alive to over-hearing bits of racist commentary, to people not quite looking you in the eye and slightly avoiding touching you. These behaviours echo through the generations.

Even so, while there's no doubt in my mind that where we lived was marked out as the 'black' house or the 'darkies' house', in my memory there is something about it that declared a presence in quite a confident way – as if to say, 'we're here'. Everybody who lived there faced a lot of racism, and around the time of the Notting Hill and Nottingham anti-black riots in 1958, our house had a couple of firebombs filled with paraffin thrown in. This caused some fire damage to two rooms at the front of the house but nothing serious as the adults dealt with it really quickly.

There was a sense of siege, but there was never a compromise in terms of the cultural practices of our lives. People had to either deal with it or not. That in itself gave me a confidence and a sense of being black. So although I'd be racially abused as half-caste and ask my mum things like, 'How come you live in a house here with us, because you're the only white person and this is where black people live?' I don't remember ever thinking of myself as other than black.

The Caribbean culture of the area felt like mine and as I got older the statement 'I'm black and I'm proud' became ideological. In June 1969 I remember walking up to the hairdresser's and saying that I wanted all my straightened hair cut off. That's when I first went natural.

SOUTHAMPTON DOCKS

My biological father, Bill, was from Guyana, and I think he arrived in London in 1947. He'd been in the RAF. Bill was a deeply damaged man because of his unfulfilled ambitions, in part because of the effects of racism denying him opportunities. He was very articulate and had wanted to come here to study to be a lawyer. He was quite attracted to anti-colonial work, Caribbean politics and the socialist movement in British Guiana, and would stand up to speak in Hyde Park. But he was not a nice man. The best thing my mum did was to get away from him – for me and for her.

When I got into political activism, the family would say, 'Oh, you're just like your father.' But my dad who grew me and who I think of as 'Dad', was from Jamaica. I used to love it when someone would arrive from the Caribbean and bring me a piece of sugar cane, tamarind, mango or fresh ackee and sing Jamaican folk songs. The Jamaica of my mind, the Jamaica of my dad's mind, and the Jamaica of my mum's mind were not the same thing. I was formed somewhere in the interstices of my fantasies, my dad's memories and my mum's false visions of Jamaica.

My dad came to England just post-Windrush, around 1949 or 1950, when he was about eighteen. He wanted to better himself and further his training as an electrician, but I don't think that happened, because when I was growing up, he always worked in car tyre factories. He smelled of rubber all the time.

I remember going to Southampton Dock as a child to meet my grandmother, Ms Dawkins, and her partner Mr Mac, as they came over on a ship from Jamaica. We drove down in my dad's car, and I had to be dressed up to meet her. I hated wearing dresses when I was a kid. Especially fancy ones. My dad would always make me wear them for special occasions. They were slightly flare-y, with fitted hips, probably sleeveless. But they always felt too tight and uncomfortable. But even so, it was really an exciting moment in the sense that I was going to meet my Jamaican grandmother for the first time!

REPLAYING REJECTION

My mum was from England, from a working-class suburb just outside London. The reason she was kicked out of her family home was multifaceted. It was about the fact she was having a black child; it was about the fact that she was a single mother; it was about the fact that she was working class and had nothing to support herself with.

Her mother never gave up on her, but her father did and chucked her out. He couldn't bear her 'betrayal' and never forgave her. He also thoroughly disliked my birth father, and there's a reason for that – he was not a nice man. But the main thing wasn't his character, it was the colour of his skin. My sense of my grandad is that he couldn't bear to look at me, and I certainly don't really remember him talking to me. When my sister, who was also black, was born in 1961, he used to embrace her, so maybe he thought it was an opportunity to make good. He died when she was two.

The paradox of all this is that by rejecting my mother he was replaying his own story. Although he was white, he was Scottish, and he was raised by his mother and his aunt in Edinburgh. What we didn't know until later was that he was actually born in St Pancras in London. His mum was unmarried, and his birth father was German. In 1906 or whenever it was, having a kid with a German was almost as bad as having a child with a black man in 1951, and his mum got thrown out of her house. My grandad was a socialist in terms of his class politics, which added another element of complexity.

When my mum was in the mother and baby unit for unmarried women, the matron had a similar view to my grandad. She had the heteronormative idea (which I guess was completely dominant at the time) that children need two parents. By suggesting that mum give me up for adoption, she fantasised that my mum would be able to get a second chance to lift herself out of the pit into which she'd fallen. My mum says that the matron liked her – so much so that she even said, 'We do have a couple. A black man and a white woman. He's a doctor, so she would have a good life. She'd have a mum and a dad, and I will bend the rules and let you meet them.' I think she may have been tempted, but she said no.

COUSIN RAY

Growing up, my best friend Ray was also mixed race. I call him my cousin, but he was more like a brother. Ray was the son of my mum's friend Paula, who she met in the mother and baby unit. They were both having black children and Ray was exactly one week younger than me. They became lifelong friends and Ray and I were together all the time. They lived in Harlesden, and we used to walk from Kilburn, through Queen's Park, Kensal Rise, to his house.

We faced a lot together. Adults would talk about us as being half-caste, or coloured. We often used to play in Paddington Recreation Ground, and one time some kids started calling us 'niggers', 'wogs', 'sambos' and 'jungle bunnies'. We tried to avoid them because we'd get in trouble if we got into fights, but it got quite nasty and they began to throw stones at us, and we threw them back and started scrapping. There was a lot of gravel and we both had grazed knees. In some senses, it was just normal kid stuff, but there's no doubt that it was racism that was firing those fights. Another time, we took on a thirteen-year-old boy who was a boxing champion for the county.

After the slum clearings in 1960 when they tore our house down, we moved from Kilburn to a rented flat in Harrow Weald. A little later on, Ray's parents came and lived in some flats just around the corner and Ray and I would then play in the countryside.

I went to school in Kilburn, which is like saying I went to school in Hackney or Brixton nowadays, but back then I was the only black child. Ray went to school in Harlesden, and he was the only black child there, too. It's easy to forget there were so few of us around. At primary school, I did fairly badly, and then suddenly in secondary school when I was around 12 or 13, something opened up and, for some reason, I came top of the class. I was moved up to an A class; meanwhile, Ray was put down into a C class, along with all of my other friends.

When we'd got into our twenties we went on different journeys for a while. Although I left school early with just two O levels, eventually I went to university. Ray went in other directions. There's something gendered about that story, which also carries over to us being the children of the so-called Windrush moment. He was troubled because he'd had quite a hard life, but when we got to middle age and he had his boys and a wife he really loved who looked after him, he began to settle down. But then he got very ill and he died.

I miss him. Ray made me feel safe in the world. He protected me, he loved me, and although he became quite a hard man to the external world for survival, he was actually also very tender, especially towards his children, his wife and his mum, before she died.

SRI LANKA

I was a late developer, academically. I couldn't read properly until I was ten, at which point I was rescued by a teacher who realised and taught me. As black children, we were belittled and not considered intelligent or able. I loved sports and I was good at them, but like many other black children, that was where I was channelled. After I got yet another detention in primary school, my teacher Mr Montague would say, 'Stand up, girl, present yourself properly. Don't you know you could be a very good leader?' I thought 'What?' But it was a different statement than 'you're good at sports' and it meant something.

After I left school, I went to work in factories, cleaning, in offices, and on the phones. Finally I got a job working as a library assistant at University College London when I was 20. I spent my time looking at all these books, but more importantly, seeing what exactly a student was. I remember thinking, 'If they can do it maybe I can.'

It was amongst those books in the library that I met my future husband, Dave, who was a student studying zoology. For his PhD, he wanted to look into a particular macaque monkey that only lives in Sri Lanka, and so we went out to live there when I was twenty-three. Being in Sri Lanka was crucial to my becoming a black feminist because it was a small island with a big sister, India, above it. It was in a complex relationship of distinguishing itself. But above all it was in Sri Lanka that I met women of colour who identified as feminist and refused to accept the idea that only white women could be feminist. It was also in Sri Lanka that I decided to try to go to university to study social anthropology.

In terms of my other politics, I'd been a socialist since I was thirteen and I had a little foray in the Young Communist League, but I wasn't happy just being in white socialist organisations so I became an anti-racist activist. I was aware I had been formed through – but not reduced by – racism. That goes back to my household, and its unashamed declaration of its presence. By the time I got to the London School of Economics university, at twenty-five in 1976, I had decided to join the Brixton Black Women's Group, started by Olive Morris, Gerlin Bean and other women who had been active in the Black Power movement.

We knew that we had to understand and declare the issues that black women were facing in the UK because these weren't yet on the agenda. We might campaign for a nursery in a local area to show people that it shouldn't be seen as separate from the workers' strike, the nurses' strike, labour struggles, the struggles for service provision and infrastructure building, political struggles and immigration controls. We, alongside other black and Asian womens groups, also campaigned against the discriminatory practice of the long-term prescription of the contraceptive Depo-Provera to black women and 'virginity tests' that women were subjected to when they tried to emigrate to the UK.

In fact it was because we recognised just how many black and Asian women's groups there were, in local communities, in labour organisations, on campuses and as sections in organisations fighting for national liberation and against neo-colonialism all over Africa, Asia, the Middle East and across the 'Third World' as we called it then, that we felt the need to start a national Black Women's organisation. So a group of sisters from these local organisations, like Haringey Black Sisters, Brixton Black Women's Group and African Red Family, a student based group, decided to start what became the Organisation for Women of African and Asian Descent and we had our first national conference in 1979 at the Abeng Centre in Brixton.

ALIENATED

Because of my work in activism I was furious but not at all surprised when I learned about the Windrush scandal. That they went round chucking people out and not letting them back in should remind us that we're in a condition of natal alienation, which, if you follow Harvard sociologist Orlando Patterson, is one of the characteristics of being an enslaved person. You are natally alienated, both from your nation of origin and your culture, however fictional that is, and you are alienated from your mother. Quite literally.

Windrush represents that in such a visceral way, because so many people affected by this Windrush scandal came on their mothers' passports. They were children and now because of this are being treated as though they are here illegally or denied entry back in. Natal Alienation!

The state has put Windrush as a placeholder for their 'hostile environment', for their attempts to deny the reverbations of colonisation, for their attempts to limit our presence and maintain us in a state of subordinated inclusion, but we have to use it as the site from which we look back and look forward. I could not be prouder to be the descendant of the Windrush generation. They literally tried to denigrate us, to make us into the abhorrent 'negro', but they've not succeeded.

IN MY BLOOD

Lenny Henry

as told to Charlie Brinkhurst-Cuff

Lenny Henry has risen from being a cult star on children's television to being one of Britain's best-known and loved personalities – who has had a crucial influence on the creation of black-centred comedy and characters. In 2018, he produced the documentary The Commonwealth Kid, *which saw him investigate his own heritage and the relationship between the Caribbean and the UK.*

In Jamaica I feel the family connection, the blood in the ground. I feel myself there.

Up until 2018, I had put a lot of time going to the African continent, talking about their problems. When I did make it back to Jamaica in March of that year to film my BBC documentary, *The Commonwealth Kid*, I was blown away by how much like Uganda or Ethiopia it was. The way the villages are set up with walks to the well to get water and the children playing outside. My parents always talked about it with pride; the farming, the city and politics. They talked about it like this big place, with big problems, and big people – not this little place with these little villages. It's a poor country.

Even if it weren't for the documentary, I would've done the journey it shows at some point in my life, to rediscover Jamaica. I first went there in 1985, with my then-wife, Dawn French. Dawn was very adventurous and so we drove all over the place. We visited the parish of St Anne, and went into the country in

Clarendon, where my family are from. We found the May Pen clock tower, where two guys were playing dominoes, and asked them if they knew where my aunty's shop was. They pointed us in the right direction, and we drove right into the bush, giving an old Jamaican lady (who looked about 900 years old) a lift. My aunty Nina was there, and she welcomed us by killing and cooking chicken for dinner.

Dawn had been to India once, but she'd never seen anything like this. There were goats running around, and all these very sharp-looking school children – who seemed much older than their age – staring at her from the bush. It was a real experience. Later, we met and stayed with Chris Blackwell, who owns the GoldenEye resort in St Mary, where Ian Fleming wrote the James Bond novels in the 1950s.

I was always interested in my black heritage. When I went to Ethiopia and Kenya for the first time, it felt like an explosion. You're plugged into the national grid, and everybody looks like you. The comedian Richard Pryor does a great skit about Africa where he says, 'People are jabbering at you and saying things because they think they know you.' You look around, and people have your nose, your eyebrows, your ears. When you go to your home country, you feel your heritage run through your veins. You suddenly come alive, I'd say 25 per cent more alive. You know why you're in that place, you live and breathe it, you feel it.

The last time I was in Jamaica, for the documentary, I went to where my mum, dad and granny used to live and found out that it was actually part of a plantation. I saw the tiny graves of my baby brothers and sisters that didn't make it to England – the kids that my mum had who died before she moved over. I even accidentally met one of my relatives when I was staying at the Half Moon Hotel in Montego Bay. One of the cleaning staff came in and said, 'Yuh name Henry? You know Winifred Henry from St Anne, Clarendon, by the clock tower?' I was like, 'What?!' It turned out we were cousins.

The whole experience made me really acknowledge that my mum had been through a lot before she left Jamaica. And I thought, 'I know why you had to get out of here.' She was so hard-working and brilliant – I know that after she had me, she went back to work the next day. My dad was brilliant too, but for different reasons. He did what guys do – get your head down, do the work, give your wife the pay packet.

THIRTEEN SHILLINGS

Adventure is what fuels diaspora people. They are making a move for the good of everybody, to prove their lot in the world and make it better. *Empire Windrush* was ten years before my mum came over to Britain and she was ready to be the first in my family to make the move. Naturally, she was pissed off that there wasn't a camera crew waiting for her when she arrived but she was under no illusions. She felt as though if she stayed in Jamaica, she would stall and die, but if we took this chance, we might just be able to turn everything around.

My uncle Clifton had written a letter from England, talking about the black country, Dudley, the amount of jobs, and how much money you could earn. At the time, my family was subsistence farming, going to market twice a week and selling their produce. But the problem was, everybody was doing it. If everybody is growing things and taking them to market, everybody is trying to undercut and there isn't any money to be made. Clifton said, 'Come to Britain, there's work and you can earn thirteen shillings a week.' They weren't earning thirteen shillings in Jamaica.

My mum and my dad, Winston, discussed it because they already had my four siblings – Beverly, Hilton, Seymour and Kay – in Jamaica. I think there were arguments, and my dad was furious at being left with the children. But she left and arrived here anyway in the mid-fifties to set up a base, while my dad Winston sold the house and wrapped up business affairs in Jamaica.

Some people were welcoming, but she was chased down the street by kids who had never seen a black person before and wanted to know where her tail was. She saw the signs in the windows saying 'No blacks, no Irish, no dogs'. But eventually she found a room in a house which an Asian family owned, and she found several jobs. She worked in a factory on machines, tube setting, or making widgets, and she made wedding cakes and dresses. She did whatever she could to get money to send for the rest of the family.

My dad travelled over with Kay in the 1960s, and then they sent for Hilton, Beverly and Seymour, who was the last to arrive.

I was born in 1958 – the first of my seven siblings to be born in the UK – as a result of an extramarital affair my mum had while my dad was still in Jamaica, as I wrote about in my BBC film *Danny and the Human Zoo*. But they went on to have two more children, Paul and Sharon, and although I knew about my mum's affair, my dad brought me up as his own.

Slowly but surely, they were able to get £3,000 to buy a house. They continued to work very hard and I rarely saw my dad – he was out at 5 a.m. and he came back at 6 at night, covered in soot from the foundry. He rarely spoke and unlike my mum, he wasn't very happy being here. He didn't like the cold and he missed home. He always put jumpers under his suit and he loved watching the West Indies cricket team on television, or listening to them on radio.

My dad died in 1977, the same year as Elvis Presley, affected by renal failure and dementia. I was only nineteen and it was tough, but it was when my mum passed away in 1998 that I was really moved. It was like somebody had pulled a big cosmic carpet away, because she was the adventurer. She was the one who said, 'I'm going to Britain, I'm going to set down roots for us all.' She'd come to school if any kids said racist things to me about being black and kick ass. When a teacher at primary school kicked me because I threw paint she showed up the next day and demanded they apologise. Mum was my hero and she protected us – she didn't back down from conflict or retreat from obstacles – she took them on and showed us by example how to persist and gradually break them down.

My older brothers were racially abused a lot. They got chased down the street by Teddy boys and had to learn how to defend themselves because they were not welcome. It was a right-wing sentiment: 'Keep Britain White' slogans were written on the walls by right-wingers in Dudley. The idea they had that black people had come over to Britain to steal everybody's jobs was pervasive even though that wasn't the case; our nurses were the best in the world, our men were strong, and we were invited to come over here and help to rebuild Britain after the war.

My parents didn't think about education very much. You were either smart or you weren't. My sister Kay was smart; she was head girl. Seymour was very smart; Hilton is smart. But we weren't given the infrastructure to get us to grammar school and university. So nobody mentioned O levels, A levels. I somehow thought that without any preparation, study or revision, I would sail through the eleven-plus. My parents knew it was coming. They wished me luck and my brother Seymour said he'd give me ten shillings if I passed. But it was too late because I hadn't done any homework, and homework is key. Embarrassingly, I didn't pass.

So instead of going to grammar school, I went to a secondary modern. I had to deal with racism all of the time. A teacher even said that I 'grew up in a sink'. If an authority figure says that, it's deep. But you grow up and you get through it. You realise there are paths to choose all the time when you're the child of the diaspora. You can go this way, or you can go that way. You can follow the bad men, and you run around on the street causing trouble and shit, or you can make something of your life, and honour your parents with your journey. I chose to make my mum proud.

COMMONWEALTH

For a lot of people in the UK, the Commonwealth is this big, abstract thing that has a whiff of slavery and empire about it. They don't want to get involved in it. It's this thing that happens over there with those 'muckety mucks' from all the different Commonwealth countries. And they aren't really sure how it benefits the people on the ground. But I wouldn't exist if it weren't for the Commonwealth, so I do see the positive side to it as well as the negative.

What I found in Jamaica, Antigua and Barbuda is that there are some pragmatic things that need to be sorted out. The Commonwealth needs to be changed and rebranded as a proper granular organisation, that helps people and facilitates aid and trade subsidies, and helps to rectify land disputes. Britain can never wash the taste of slavery out of its mouth, so it would help to make up for that legacy.

Beyond that, I believe that your children are your legacy, and if you don't invest in your legacy, and help them to get through the difficult times, you're not doing your job. My parents were involved in the battle to survive in a Britain that didn't really want them to be here. The battle to raise their kids and not have them out in the streets causing trouble. The battle to keep them clothed and fed. The battle to be part of a community.

My daughter Billie's adopted. We love her and she's our kid, and she's chaotic, and sometimes she talks about her Caribbean heritage, and sometimes she doesn't. But there's a life journey with being adopted. When she decides to take on the great detective work, I hope I'm there to help her, just as my parents helped me.

FAMILY TREE

Sharon Frazer-Carroll

Sharon Frazer-Carroll is an international education and training expert, higher education psychology lecturer, psychodynamic counsellor and Pan-Africanist. Her mother grew up in Antigua and her mysterious father, whose family tree she is only just discovering, was Jamaican.

When I was about nine years old, part of the ceiling in our old Victorian house fell in, taking the MFI cabinet, state-of-the-art stereo system and wooden table with it to the floor below. Despite the devastation and destruction, Mum laughed. The threat of the sizeable bricks which had narrowly missed us didn't faze her at all, and the financial predicament brought by the downfall simply seemed a joke to us children as Mum described the fright with which we'd jumped up when we heard the first lumps of plaster fall.

'Lard,' she'd exclaimed, throwing her head back and covering her mouth with her hand. 'You ever see sudden lacka dat? Brick start to fire like volcano a shoot larda and Sheran jump up lacka fire cracker na she behine, the brick coulda never catch her.'

The thought of bricks coming down like volcanic lava and me outrunning them as if I'd had a fire cracker in my behind brought *Tom and Jerry* to mind. All fear dissipated as we children jumped about, joking and imitating each other. Making fun of herself, Mum said: 'Even me wid me one foot jump up an shape one side like me ready fi do quadrille.' For the first few years of my life, I'd never really noticed that Mum had a bad leg, but the thought of her accelerating from having a slight limp to being fleet-footed seemed amazingly funny, even though I had no idea that the quadrille was a dance.

Mum was a great orator, always brimming with stories from her past. Her vivacious descriptions, metaphors and songs brought life to every tale and evoked laughter at many a tragedy. She would retell her stories on many occasions, each time with renewed vigour and emphasis. I remember my little brother and I joining the adults as they listened and doubling up with laughter till we were out of breath, holding our bellies and crying.

Growing up in east London during the sixties and seventies with my mother, older sister and younger brother, I had a great childhood, with enduring memories – full of hilarious, horrendous and exciting times. Ours was a matriarchal household. Mum ruled the home with a firm rod and frequent explanations of why it was important to keep order when there was no man around. Educational attainment was important, and Mum stressed that if we were going to get anywhere in life we needed to look and learn. Bible lessons, prayers and proverbs were a staple part of our emotional diet. If a workperson came to the house, we all knew that we needed to watch what they did, in case there was a skill that could be picked up. As a result, I learned to paint, tile, wallpaper and change a plug in my primary years.

'Watch and learn,' Mum would say. 'Pick up whatever you can, whenever you can; you never know when it will come in useful. Don't mek anybody have to tell you fi look. You all need to learn to be man and woman – I don't care if you tell me that I want you to be hermaphrodite or whatever you call it. You don't know how life will turn out. Prepare for every eventuality and that way nobody can tek advantage of you.'

Mum often talked of 'back a yard', a term meaning 'home'. She told us she was born in a small village in a place called Antigua. Her childhood home had been a land with palm trees, golden sand, crystal-clear water and blue skies. She talked of playing with conch shells, eating mangoes and searching for mermaids. 'One day when you are all grown I will return home,' she'd explained. She stressed that she had come to England to make a better life for us, so she could earn money and give us opportunities she hadn't had.

I never saw any pictures of Antigua, so it was difficult to visualise, but I fancied it must have been like the island featured in the *Robinson Crusoe* film or like the vividly coloured places I'd seen in the Saturday morning cartoons of *Gulliver's Travels*. It was a fantasy land; nobody at school recognised it as country or island. When I told people at school where Mum had come from, friends and teachers would say, 'I've never heard of that place, is it in Jamaica?' It was often easier to say yes: it would cure the quizzical looks and stop the questions for which I had no answer. By the time I was seven or eight I learned to say that my father was from Antigua too. If I replied that he came from

Jamaica, as I believed he did, they'd ask me where and I didn't have an answer. It was a difficult course to navigate, but I was gradually learning the way.

Mum told us of the warm weather and carefree lifestyle. She taught us to play a card game called 'wappy', which meant you could slap the hand of the losing opponents if you won. She took care to ensure that we all knew the names of her siblings and helped us write frequent letters to relatives back home. I wrote most frequently to my aunty Irose, who Mum said 'was over the postal service' (meaning she worked there) at the time. As she taught me to fill in the blue airmail envelopes, it intrigued me that there was no door number. The envelope was simply addressed with my aunt's name, then Grays Hill, Antigua.

At Christmas we hunted for cards featuring snow, as Mum explained that they didn't have snow where she had come from, so her brothers and sisters in Antigua had never seen it. Determined not to lose family ties, I remember her testing my younger brother and me on her siblings' names from a very young age. Mum was the third child of nine. There was Wellyn, Irose, then Mummy, who they referred to as Lonnie. She was followed by Yevonne, Dixon, Aurora, Roy, Son and Geraldine. 'Son's not a name,' I remember my brother and I exclaiming. 'That's what everybody call him,' Mum had said, 'His real name is Roosevelt.' This had resulted in raucous laughter from my brother and me, who asked if he got teased. Mum had smiled and explained that many people in her day were named after famous people in books or politics, so it hadn't been unusual for her brother to share his name with a US president. We stuck with calling him 'Uncle Son' after that, which now seems a bit ambiguous, but it worked for us at the time.

Mum would often call out the name of her parents in day-to-day life. Their names also became firmly etched in my consciousness from as far back as I can remember. I believe this might be a way of keeping your loved ones in your heart when you've travelled such a long way away from home. At times where most people might say 'goodness, this is difficult' or 'I wonder how I'm going to manage this', Mum would instead say 'me mudda Pearl Peters and me farda Percy Peters', as if somehow this gave her strength.

She prided herself on her standards, always aiming for quality and striving to progress. She was careful to warn me away from 'bad company' and encouraged us to 'hold our heads high'. She'd tell us that there were three classes of people: 'aristocrat, democrat and dutty rat'. She had no faith that I could identify and avoid 'dutty rats', so kept me close by her. I wasn't allowed to stay after school for extracurricular activities like netball or rounders. Mum would say, 'Netball and rounders won't get you anywhere, education and qualifications will. The best place for you is where I can see you. Go and do your book and, if you get bored of that, look for a cupboard to clean out. One day you will thank me.' From the stories I picked up from the adults talking around me, I understood that Mum had originated from a more privileged background than many. My aunt Aurora referred to it as a 'well-to-do' family with what was 'a big house dem times and a big yard and servants', setting them apart from most other people on the island in the 1920s.

My grandfather had been overseer for the road-building that was taking place in Antigua. 'He attended to the administration in the office and supervised and managed the labourers and tradespeople from the height of his strapping horse,' Mum explained. It was a really important job as it enabled travel from one part of the island to another and supported business development in the country. My grandmother was described by my Mum as 'a tall beautiful woman with a peach-like complexion and two long plaits that fell either side of her face'. Mum didn't talk much of her during my childhood but did tell me that she had a sister named Theresa and that her mother (my great-grandmother) was called Tunka, which I've found out has Ghanaian origins. I was also told that I walked like my grandmother, with my head tilted to one side, and in later years Mum would stand with her sister and muse at the similarity: 'The chip doesn't fly far from the block,' they would say.

Colonisation had left its marks and colourism ran rife in the island. Consequently, Mum's darker complexion did not bring her favour with her mother, and she told stories of scoldings laced with references to colour. Mum's good nature and considerateness, however, earned her the reputation as 'the kindest of the children' and I'd hear this reference in later years when she would pay for my aunt to learn nursing, look after sick relatives and cook for everyone passing by. Although I often probed to find out more about the names and nature of my grandparents, Mum would explain that things back then were different, you couldn't ask big people questions, they would tell you to 'go bout you business'. She was telling me as much as she knew.

When Mum was about eight, her parents split up. Prone to excessive drinking, my grandfather's temper resulted in my grandmother leaving the home. The family's wealth stemmed from my grandfather's work so 'Mamma', as my mum referred to her mother, did not feel she could take the children with her. Fleeing the house meant that she was without a home, and it felt cruel to rip the children from their comfortable surroundings where servants could at least tend to their physical needs. Mum described this time to me as 'the start of the great downfall'. With my grandmother gone, my grandfather's temper turned on the other inhabitants of the home and within a year both the servants and the children felt the situation was intolerable. The information shared about what happened to each of her siblings here is patchy, and I learned much from discussions between my aunt and my mum vociferously debating the past over pots of Saturday soup. From what I could gather, my uncle Wellyn was able to go to work as the oldest of the children and my aunty Irose married into wealth and inherited responsibilities over the postal service at the time. Aunty Aurora was adopted by a fair-skinned family who saw her privately educated and musically trained.

My mum was neither old enough to marry nor young enough to be a prime candidate for adoption and sought refuge in the cane fields, which bemused me when she told me about the situation.

What did she eat? What did she wear? This was inconceivable and much worse than any of the fairy tales like *Heidi* or *The Prime of Miss Jean Brodie*, which I concerned myself with. In the fields, my mum scraped by, finding work by helping out villagers who wanted odd jobs doing, like fetching, carrying and cleaning. She talked of scaling mango trees for food, bathing in the sea and using grass for toilet paper. When I asked about cups for drinking, she'd say 'Wa me know bout cup? Dem times people would use ole can or cup their han.' When I asked about mirrors, she'd tell me they would look in water. Toothbrushes consisted of a rag with carbolic soap. This was far beyond my imagination. A woman that used to pass by, Mrs Benjamin, gave Mum a Bible which she used to teach herself to read and write, building on the little she already knew. Every day Mum would copy a word or two out of the Bible using a stick and drawing in the sand, and when Mrs Benjamin passed she'd ask her what the word was. Eventually she found she could read whole scriptures.

Not everyone was as kind as this. When Mum was about eleven a woman took her in from the fields as a house cleaner on the promise of giving her food and somewhere to sleep. Her bed turned out to be under the bed with the dogs. 'When de big daag dem come in dem just shake off de dutty water pan you, and when dem finish dem cock up dem foot an piss pan you. You haf fi run fine water fi wash. Dis was real hard life.' She would shake her head and laugh, often reminding us not to complain about the minor problems we had. Mum was open about the physical and sexual abuse she suffered during this time in households such as these, 'Plenty time, woman husband tek you fi wife,' she'd say, 'me haf fi run back to cane field fi safety.'

Going between houses and the fields and, on at least one occasion, trying to go back to her original home, Mum made it through her early teen years. Things were yet to get worse however. When she was around eighteen, a hurricane hit Antigua and a piece of wood from one of the buildings flew into her upper thigh, rendering her unconscious with the pain. When she woke she'd been taken in by the Salvation Army, who would be responsible for nursing her to health. They sapped her leg daily, used poultices and balms made from arrowroot, aloes, cerasee and other local plants. It would take over five years before she could walk again. During this time Mum said she received no visitors. She had a constant refrain that 'rather than look bout me, some a me family does tek the far far road round so dem no pass me na de hospital'. I never understood why family hadn't come to help look after her, but she would advise, 'You can't depend on nobody but God, man will fail, God will prevail.' In later years, relatives that visited the house said that they never knew. Either way, I saw the pain in her eyes and felt the same in my heart. Hugging her, I would often say, 'I would have come to visit you if I was there, Mum.'

Mum got married shortly after coming out of hospital and gave birth to my big sister in 1955. She frequently talked of the unreasonable behaviour she endured from her husband during this marriage; for example, at the wedding reception held at their home, he showed his objection to the visiting of her Christian

114

friends by hanging his dirty underwear on a line across the doorway. His continued poor conduct meant that all the guests left soon after arrival. 'Lawd I was embarrassed, you see . . . de ting dem just flap in de people face as dem come true de door.' Mum said she was so embarrassed that she never went back to see those friends again and consequently lost all contact.

TAKING IN SEA

I don't remember Mum sharing very much about her journey over to the UK; however she did say that it was long. She said that she and the other passengers wondered whether they would ever see land again. I can imagine the fear, risk and level of enterprise that must have been necessary to make the trip, particularly in my mum's case, given that she was travelling with my sister, a young child of only three and a half. I understand that during my mum's journey, they believed the boat was sinking as it was taking in water, and it was necessary to dock at the nearest European country from where the crossing could be continued. The passage should have taken four weeks, but in Mum's case it was longer because of the break in the journey. Mum's husband travelled to England first so that he could find accommodation and Mum followed after. I seem to remember Mum telling me that her ticket cost around £30. 'That was plenty money in those days,' she'd explain.

She'd worked cleaning houses, doing dressmaking and picking

cotton to scrape together the money. Friends also clubbed together to contribute. That helped explain the barrels we would put together in my house to send home. Sending barrels 'home' was a common West Indian practice. We bought the barrels from a travel shop in Balls Pond Road, Dalston, which was about fifteen minutes' drive from our house, and would fill it with things like clothes, shoes, corned beef and salt. Mum explained, 'You need to remember where you're coming from, as well as where you're going to. Some people don't even have two coppers to rub together. Wind knock them down before them have a skirt or a blouse fu put ahn.' I could comprehend the idea that some people were not as lucky as us and we should try to help them if we could. This was another lesson that Mum instilled.

When they arrived at the docks in England in 1958, Mum and my sister got off the ship to immediately be met by a group of skinheads. Mum would often talk of her greeting. 'Mi look up and mi see a group of shave head bwoy.' She later understood these were skinheads. 'Me see dem a look pan we side-eye and when me realise a chase dem a chase we, me pick up me foot and me start to run, you see – is we life we a run fa, you know. Lard what a ting.' Mum was wearing a long maxi dress as had been the fashion in those days; she'd told my sister to get under her skirt and not to get out until she told her to 'me sure dem catch some people behind ah we, but me put arn a running, you see. That was my welcome to Britain.'

LONDON LIFE

Mum's dreams of being welcomed were shattered. Like the other Caribbeans who had made the journey, she believed she was coming to the 'Motherland' to work. I remember asking Mum how she had heard about the jobs in England and she explained that the posters had been put up all over the place and flyers were so plentiful they were blowing around in the breeze. 'They were begging for our help, we wanted to earn, but it also felt like we were doing a service.' It had never crossed her mind that the people of England wouldn't like black people, or that she wouldn't be welcome. On reflection, the degree of shock is understandable to me. In the West Indies there was systemic and ingrained prejudice which played out in colourism and white people being revered; it wasn't overt in the same way it was in Britain. People actually did talk about there being gold on the streets, and while my mum knew not to take that literally, she did think it was going to be easier to settle and make a living than it turned out to be.

When one day Mum's husband directed his aggression towards my sister, Mum decided she would play it quiet, pack a small bag from the night before and leave the house as soon as he went to work in the morning. Mum would declare, 'Me go through too much hardship in life to see anybody ill-treat my children dem. Never again!' She would brush her hands together as if slapping off the dust of the past to show the finality of her words. I can only guess how petrified Mum must have felt. Having only recently immigrated she didn't yet know anybody and was unfamiliar with London.

She talked of the cold and the wind and the tiring process of knocking from door to door. 'I thought I would never be able to rest again,' she told me. 'Me can't count the doors me knock pon.' Switching between her English and West Indian accents she would demonstrate how she'd knocked and said 'Excuse me, Miss, I'm wondering if you or anyone you know has any rooms to let,' only to then have a door shut in her face or somebody 'fire spit pass you' and turn around. Some of the people said things like 'Sorry this isn't a zoo, we don't take monkeys here,' others saved you the trouble of knocking, clearly displaying signs which read 'NO BLACKS, NO IRISH, NO DOGS'.

'Tears fill up my eyes,' Mum would say, 'but I persevered. Who don't sink *mus* swim. I wasn't dead yet, so I had to carry on.' Eventually she struck upon a house which was rented out to black people. Several families lived in each room of the house, so there were already ten or twelve adults when she arrived. Seeing Mum with a small child and having all experienced similar obstacles in finding accommodation, they agreed to take her in until she could find work. 'At last, I had my own quarters,' she said, which literally was a quarter of a whole room, separated by curtains so that four families could live in it.

In that house, Mum made a new type of family. 'There were people from every kina island. Everybody mix up, Grenadian, Dominican, Jamaican, Trinidadian . . . We would all get together and tell our different stories, and then find out we had all of these things in common. We would laugh at each other's accents and try to copy each other. We sit down and joke together and get on real good.' Mum said this house was where she really learned to cook. I was surprised that many of the dishes I'd grown up eating weren't native to Antigua. 'Antiguans are well known for their jerk chicken, fungee and ducana, but most of what I cook I learn from Jamaicans, Trinidadians and other people. After that I learn to use trial and error.' We both would laugh loudly here as we each conjured up images of the many experimental dishes she'd trialled. She was always one for learning new skills.

Mum then needed to find work to pay for her room, and eventually she fell upon a Jewish woman, Mrs Betjeman, who gave her a house-cleaning job and allowed my sister to stay with her at work. Mrs Betjeman said Jewish people had also had a hard time in Britain and understood when somebody needed a helping hand. Mum decided she would do her best at this job; if Mrs Betjeman told her to clean the kitchen, she'd clean the kitchen and the toilet. If she told her to do the living room, she did the stairs and the front of the house too. 'Always go the extra mile,' she'd tell me, 'a little extra goes a long, long way'. Mrs Betjeman liked her so much that she paid her extra.

In the meantime, Mum's husband had knocked and knocked on doors himself, until he tracked her down. However the other members of the household stopped him from coming in. 'If you take her, you'll have to take us too, because we're one family now,' they said. Disgusted, he'd asked for the clothes she and my sister were wearing when they left the house. Mum said, 'He even asked for some clothes pegs which he said I'd taken in my bundle.'

COW FOOT AND SUGAR LUMPS

Mum worked 24/7 to ensure we had the best life she could give us. Often times were tough, but she found much consolation in Christianity and was a devout and leading member of the New Testament Church of God which we attended in Stoke Newington, Church Street. Church on Sunday was a whole-day affair and could last for four to five hours. There were black and white people at the church and all sang loudly accompanied by tambourines and drums, which was very different to the Catholic church around the corner to where we lived. I remember how surprised my brother and I were when Mum was said to have first received the Holy Spirit. Getting in the spirit meant that people shook and spoke in a foreign tongue that nobody understood. They would sometimes pass out and other church members looked after them. This was something that Mum and some of the other 'elders in the church' were familiar with; however it was not something my brother and I had seen before, resulting in concern and then amusement as we got used to the routine.

When my sister was old enough to go to school, Mum took a job in a sugar factory in Tottenham Hale. For years later, she talked of the surprise she'd had when the white women she worked with told her not to answer back, but just to spit in the sugar if she was ever upset with the way the supervisor shouted at her. Growing up, we weren't ever allowed to eat sugar lumps.

Alongside her job in the factory, Mum continued her cleaning work, by which time word of her efficiency had spread. Fed up of renting and depending on others, Mum was determined to buy her own house. 'Beg water cyan cook cow foot,' she would counsel. Meaning you can't bank on accomplishing ambitious things when the resources you need have to be given to you as a favour. I later understood the correlation, as cow foot was a dish that required stewing for one to two hours with a pressure cooker and four to five hours without, which meant lots of water was required. She worked night and day and threw *pardners** to save enough money for a mortgage on this first house in Mount Pleasant Lane in Clapton. It was in the 1960s, before I was born, and houses then were about £3,000, which was a lot of money. Renting out rooms helped others who still found it hard to find lodgings and her with mortgage payments in these early days. Mum met my father in the corner shop called Giffy's in 1962 and this house in Clapton became my first home.

THE FATHER

I was three and a half when my sister found the letter in my father's coat pocket saying that he had a wife and five children in

---

* Collective saving schemes used by Carribean families.

Jamaica. The woman in the letter complained that he'd been in England for several years now and wondered why it was taking so long to find accommodation for his existing family to join him. I was standing on his feet, which he tapped up and down to make me laugh, and Mum was doing the ironing behind me. I remember my sister, who was about nine, passing the letter over the ironing board and Mum saying something like 'Why you go in big people pocket, you trying to mash the relationship up?' Mum was devastated at the lies she'd been told; my father had promised to marry her, and I remember the uproar as she threw something at his head and somebody scooped me up to safety from behind. That was the last time I saw him.

The deception Mum had experienced in her relationship with my father meant that I was not allowed to mention him growing up, although there was often discussion in earshot. 'I am your mother and your father,' she would remind me, 'no uncle, aunt or friend has ever helped, it's God and me alone that must do everything.' This was true as far as I was concerned. I had lots of people I called Aunty out of politeness – it was customary to do that in West Indian families – but there were no helping hands as far as I could see. I consequently blocked all thoughts of a father from my mind; my life seemed happy enough without one and he had contributed nothing to my wellbeing. I didn't allow myself to wonder whether he had siblings, what his parents were like or where he was. It was easier to pretend he had never existed.

It was to my surprise then, at the age of fifty-three, at least a decade after I had lost my mum, that the notion of a father would re-enter my life. My daughter Micha suggested that we take a 23andMe DNA test to find out about our genetic make-up. It involved filling a tube with saliva, which I found a bit gross, but we did it together and I was excited at the prospect. The results said I was 66 per cent sub-Saharan African, 17 per cent South Asian and 17 per cent European (with preliminary traces from other regions); this was broadly consistent with my suspicions. I was not aware that the test provided reports on health and traits and was particularly surprised to see that they could connect you with people who had taken the test and shared some portion of your DNA. I found there were 1,200 individuals listed as DNA relatives (which they called first to fifth cousins). I'd never imagined people in the world were so connected.

I was even more startled to find that amongst the list was a first cousin (i.e. a close DNA relative) called Ralston who originated from Jamaica. Both of my mum's parents come from Antigua, so this rang immediate alarm bells. Ralston was as curious as I was to find out how we might be related. We were both under the impression that we knew all our close relatives. In the strangest of email exchanges, we introduced ourselves. I had lots to say about myself but knew only a handful of things about my biological father, all of which had been collected from discussions around me, rather than with me. I knew he was a Jamaican 'coolie'*, was

---

* A term used to refer to Asian indentured labourers – often regarded as offensive.

referred to as Mr Willie (although that could be a first or last name), had a wife and five children who lived for a time in Jamaica, was in the UK at least between 1964 and 1967, worked on the 76 bus from Tottenham, sat on his feet and was the first person to tell my mum 'If you want to know a man, look at his parents.'

Somehow these details rang a bell with Ralston, who said that his mum and aunt were about my age and their father was called William. Ralston was able to share a photo, which I instantly recognised, and to tell me that my father's name was Albert Williams. His mother and aunt were Albert's children (and my half-siblings); however, they could only remember seeing him a handful of times. They also knew of the third family in Jamaica that my mother had read about in the letter but didn't have further details; however it was a funny feeling having a name for this man after all this time.

Several months later, a friend called Sherry, who growing up had held a Saturday job with me working in libraries and was also interested in ethnic composition, suggested I do an Ancestry test for a more detailed breakdown. Further to this I received a more comprehensive analysis of the sub-Saharan African component of my genetic make-up, while my South Asian and European elements stayed the same. I also found that this test had thrown up a further first cousin, despite there being a much smaller number of connections (seventy-nine). This relative was female and intro-duced herself as Diane. On seeing the name and photograph Diane confirmed that Albert was her uncle, and brother to her father Alvin. She explained that she too had not known her father very well but was aware that the brothers had been close. A deluge of information followed; in an email she said:

> Your father was one of about 8 children, they are all gone now. Our grandparents come from Savana-La-Mar in the parish of Westmoreland. Westmoreland is south of St James. The parish of St James is famous for Montego Bay. I believe that the family lived on Williams Street in Savana-La-Mar, before moving to St Catherine after our grandfather died. In St Catherine they lived on a hill named Dam Head.

Diane seemed a lovely woman who I immediately got on with, albeit by email. She sent me her photo and told me that Albert had originally been married to a lady she referred to as 'Aunty Daisy' who had passed away in 2012. Together they had five daughters (Lorna, Pauline, Audrey, Marlene, Doreen) and a son (Albert Jr). He was born on 30 June 1922 to Edwin Williams and Caroline Williams-Brown and died in May 1991 at Diane's father's home. She joined me up to a family tree going back several generations where I found details of 236 blood relatives. Most of the work had been done by a cousin called Tonya-Rose in Canada who was a historian, had logged birth and death certificates and made it her job to speak with and collect details of my family's lives. Albert's parents had been indentured workers who it was believed had come to Jamaica from Bombay. There was even a Williams family Facebook group where pictures and updates where shared. There were pictures of ancestors playing with children and picking fruit, and current photos of children and grandchildren. In a matter of weeks, I'd gone from knowing nothing about this side of the family to being completely overwhelmed with information. This inspired me to find out more about my mother's history; it seemed I had much work to do on this side.

A PSYCHOLOGIST DOCTOR

Mum was determined to work from within the home while we were growing up. She didn't care to let us out of her sight, forgoing child minders, play centres or youth clubs. She would say she wanted to protect me from the streets of Hackney, the Kray twins and the serial killer Myra Hindley, who was incarcerated at Holloway Prison, not far away. Resourceful as ever, she turned her hand to all sorts: training as a hairdresser, working as a dressmaker, doing millinery, providing herbal treatments, baking and decorating wedding cakes. When we moved to Stamford Hill we occupied a big house with a basement, so we could have blues parties where you could buy curry rice and a drink for £1.50, with Rastafarians simply settling for plain rice which we sold at a discount price. People would drink shots of rum and other spirits. I remember Mummy getting invitations printed out which we would give out in Ridley Road market and asking our black friends at school to pass them to their parents. Party day would always be fun; we'd try on new outfits, organise music, cook black pudding and make meat patties, all the time laughing and spoiling several batches before we perfected our recipes.

It was a lively house with visitors always dropping in to talk and for something to eat. Few people had cars, and the black community lived close together, so people were always passing by. We all had our own bedrooms but would naturally congregate in the living area where we'd watch television, play games and help Mum cook and sew. We had all the fashions of the time: jewellery, clothes, casual skirts, bow blouses and platform shoes. Staying up late through the night, Mum would put her sewing and design skills to best use, making me a new outfit almost every day. When I was older, after she'd got her hairdressing qualification, she would do my hair too. I felt very privileged and lucky.

Mum wanted me to be a doctor and I still feel some disappointment that I didn't make the grade, despite the fact that my environment wasn't the sort in which a medical student would necessarily flourish. Cleaning and decorating the house always seemed to take priority and big blocks of time over several days were taken up with church meetings of one type or another. Thinking back, this is understandable as Mum hadn't been fortunate enough to be put through a formal education system so couldn't have known all that was required. One day I remember her saying, 'Sheri, you still studying your book? You're sixteen now and all the time you a study, study. So what happen? You hard head?'

In winter we children had more freedom. The darker evenings meant Mum went to bed earlier, often as early as 5.30 p.m., although at the other end she'd also rise with the sun. Often the day's meals would be cooked, covered and refrigerated by 6.30 a.m., which meant Mum could work throughout the day and still get a full home-cooked dinner on the table by 4.30 p.m., straight after school. By the age of sixteen her early bedtimes turned into a bonus as I could start studying early, put rollers in my hair and have boyfriends over, which Mum said was OK as long as they left by 10 p.m. Summer nights were more difficult because there always seemed to be jobs to do when Mum was up.

Ultimately, I achieved nine O levels (now called GCSEs), although I got an E in French and maths which I independently retook about five times. Six of my grades were As and Bs, and although this was good attainment for my school, these grades weren't good enough to become a doctor. I gained a reputation as 'one of the clever girls'; however I remember the great sense of failure and my attempts at scraping over the grades on my certificate, so I could rewrite them and make Mum think I had done better than I had. But then I distinctly remember seeing a film in which somebody worked as a psychologist. They were wearing a white coat and worked in a hospital, so I thought that might be an alternative career. I studied social sciences and specialised in psychology at Middlesex University, a discipline which wasn't as common as it is these days and which few people had heard of. It was the 1980s and Maureen Lipman was doing her best to popularise landline telephones along with the word 'ology' in a British Telecom advert. When I graduated, I remember Mum saying to her friends, proudly, 'She's a *psychologist* doctor,' which made me squirm a little but seemed to make Mum happy.

I'd found it difficult at Middlesex to begin with. I remember almost turning back at the gates when I saw how few black people were there. I'd attended Skinners' Company School for girls in Hackney and moved on to Kingsway Princeton College in King's Cross, both of which had a strong black presence. It was not uncommon for white girls to perm their hair to form Afros, use black lingo and listen to reggae in order to fit in. The journey to university took about half an hour in my gold-brown Datsun, and the change in scenery as I entered the green belt was huge. There were just three black women and one black man in my cohort of over 300 students, two of whom were mature students. Together with the large building and open environment, everything had felt odd. We started an Afro-Caribbean society, where I took the role of social secretary. This brought us into contact with the handful of black students in other years and across the other campuses and allowed some familiarity and solidarity. I supposed this was a little like how Mum must have felt when she joined the church. Black students were so scarce that we had to persuade some of the white students to join in order to gain sufficient numbers to qualify as a society.

I met my husband, Geoff, when I left university and went to work. My sister had taken me up to Haringey Education Service to do a typing test, which led to a temporary job in a Youth Training and Education Centre. Geoff was a senior manager at the centre and was thoughtful, quiet and gentle, which attracted me as the polar opposite to my outgoing, gregarious family. In addition, he was twelve years older than me, which I thought would make him more sensible and steadier than the black boyfriends of my own age. He was white and came from a little village called Silverton in Devon, leading to many intriguing visits to the countryside. We bird-watched and played chess and spent endless hours watching films. I remember us having lengthy conversations about whether our age difference and colour would cause future difficulties. I'd previously been quite political at university having grown up on the edge of the Black Power movement and in an age where racism was prevalent. Mum and my brother, who I lived at home with at the time, embraced him however, and we went on to have three children – Pascale, Micha and Nathan.

WHERE TO FROM HERE?

'They should write a story about my life,' Mum would say. Back then I wondered who would want to know her 'commonplace' stories, often used to highlight how good my life was. I shirked away from them, and tales went in one ear and out the other. I wish I had paid more attention. I now find myself having to piece together tiny bits of information in order to understand my lineage and gather my ancestral history. My husband was working in Uganda last year and has recently talked of how much more informed individuals there were about their family connections and history, even though it was not always documented. 'People can tell you exactly how they're connected to other family members, even when describing distant relations,' he said. For me this emphasised the broken lineage essentially caused through colonisation.

Inspired by the extensive family tree on my father's side I've begun researching my mother's ancestral line. However, remaining members of my mother's generation are now in their eighties and nineties, suffering from dementia and Alzheimer's, so further opportunities to reconstruct the ancestral line are likely to soon be lost. DNA companies provide some opportunity to gain puzzle pieces and I have begun reaching out to relatives on my maternal side to find others eager to make headway on our puzzles.

Reaching back yet further, government records may hold clues. However, records for slaves in Antigua were poor and no records of ethnicity or country of birth were kept, making tracing even more difficult than might be expected. Recent research has led to me finding some hope in the investigation of Moravian Church (the most prominent church in East Africa and the Caribbean) records which apparently exist for the years between 1757 and 1833. Antigua was the 'seedbed for evangelization for the rest of the Caribbean'. By 1798, for example, there had been 8,596 Moravian baptisms in Antigua versus 315 in the much larger island of Jamaica. I have some hope that I can identify some individuals through this route.

My mother's journey is my inspiration. I remember her working for us from dusk till dawn and still hear her voice on a daily basis. 'I didn't swim over sea for you to turn out to be nothing,' she would say. 'Never stop trying, this tree may buckle, but it will not break.'

In my weakest hours she provides motivation; I remember all she went through and how she pressed on till the end.

By the time I had my children in the 1990s, Mum's leg had become weak and she was in a wheelchair. Even then she'd come over to my house to sit up with the babies, so I could get some sleep. She'd still cook and tidy up, using her walking stick to pull and push whatever she couldn't reach. She offered comfort and guidance, teaching me to talk constantly to the children, well before they could understand, and showing me how to exercise the patience that new parents often lack. I remember once asking her why she let my eldest daughter Pascale rip up all her papers and ransack her well-made bed when I hadn't been allowed to do that when I was a child. 'Me never know better,' she had answered. 'You do the best you can, whenever you can. I wasn't perfect, but I did my best. You will do a little better, but it won't be perfect either, your children will exceed you, but it may not be enough. But soon . . . soon after that, it will all be all right.'

ASPIRATION AND AMBITION

Catherine Ross

as told to Charlie Brinkhurst-Cuff

Catherine Ross is the co-founder of the UK's first National Caribbean Heritage Museum, alongside her daughter Lynda Burrell. A former accountant, lawyer and teacher, she is passionate about preserving British black history and counteracting the pervasive narrative of black underachievement. She moved to England from St Kitts in 1958 and views herself as a child of Windrush.

We're good in our family at making you feel a million dollars for your achievements. Our sense of aspiration and hard work has carried us across the ocean and beyond.

I must have had twenty different jobs and three or four different careers since my working life began in 1973. Accountant, lawyer, teacher, business consultant, museum founder. I succeeded in all of them, but I started the UK's first national Caribbean Heritage Museum in 2015 after I retired because I wanted to share the idea that black people can achieve amazing things.

When you get to a certain age you start thinking about the future, but for me, that also meant remembering my mum and dad's achievements as individuals. They raised nine children, migrated to a new country, stayed resilient despite the tough experiences of discrimination and racism, and were always keen to let others know they had a history, heritage and culture from their small island home of St Kitts. They qualified in new skills, learned new social customs and helped their children adjust, achieve and astound not just others but themselves. They have left a legacy.

There's so much that should be written about their early lives: how they made ends meet, that my dad was the first Methodist lay preacher and my mum used to cook for people in the community to make sure they had a good meal. There were so many firsts in our family and I realised there must be firsts in other Caribbean families too.

I thought I'd potter around with the project, but after my daughter Lynda got involved, it became much bigger than that. She has run her own business in the fashion and beauty sector and her creativity and skill has turned the idea of a small local museum into a national one. She came up with the idea of having a 'museum without walls'.

We have presented exhibitions on black identity, the Windrush generation, nine nights, the fifty-two genres of music that black people have created, or contributed to since 1948, and Caribbean Christmas traditions. Many people visit our exhibitions more than twice, and bring along friends at subsequent visits. They want to tell their story, to fill in the gaps we have in information and enhance the work we do, so it really has become a 'community museum'.

We got our break on local news and TV but our greatest achievements so far are that we have held a number of exhibitions at Westminster Abbey, the House of Commons and the Victoria and Albert Museum. These are places that rarely see black people engaged in heritage work, telling their story and presenting history in which they feature and take centre stage. Our museum exists because for too long the contribution of Caribbeans to the UK has been hidden or been written out of the public record. We are putting this right.

Both of my parents are from St Kitts. My dad, Allan, was a country boy from the village of Old Road and my mum, Mary, came from Parson's Ground village. St Kitts was the first Caribbean country to be colonised by the British in 1623 and Old Road is where they all landed.

By the time they married and I was born, they lived in Basseterre, the capital of St Kitts. My dad drove a truck for the country's Public Works Department and my mum was a homemaker, cooking, baking and sewing. My dad was quite a good boxer, but my mum made him give it up – and literally threw his towel in the ring, thus ending the fight and his career. They were well off and had a large breeze-block-built house rather than a wooden one, and a lot of land. My dad's workers lived in wooden houses in our yard.

I lived in St Kitts for seven years and it was a great life. We never wanted for anything and I have a sense of everything being in place. I only remember small things, like having a tricycle and being the envy of other children, learning to knit fishing nets and being taken on my dad's shoulders down to the sea through the cotton fields to bathe every day, because they thought the salt water was good for your bones.

My parents decided to come to the UK when the British government invited Caribbeans to help rebuild England after the war.

Even though they had everything they had ever wanted, we moved because they wanted to expose us to a different culture. My older sister came over first, in 1956, to become a nurse. After she had reported back that everything was great, my dad followed in 1957 to secure a house for the family, and my mother and I came in October 1958. I have nine siblings – not all by the same parentage, but as my dad said, 'So long as they're your mum's, they're mine too.' I only became aware that my three older brothers weren't his when I turned fourteen.

My journey to the UK on the SS *Montserrat* was fantastic because mum was ill, which meant everyone felt sorry for us and spoiled us. Because we came by ship we were able to run riot. Even the sailors took us under their wings. The journey seemed to take for ever, but I was having fun so it didn't matter. It could have been as short as ten days or as long as three weeks, the only thing that mattered to me at the age of seven was that I was having a good time. There were two foods we ate while onboard which I've liked for the rest of my life: large, sweet, bright red apples which filled the palm of my hand, and crusty loaves of bread. Even now on a Saturday, I'll head straight to the fresh bread aisle at the supermarket, and eat half of a French stick on my journey home.

After we arrived in Nottingham, in the East Midlands, we made ourselves open to trying new things. My dad worked for British Rail, and when my youngest sibling started school, my mum became a cleaner and then an auxiliary nurse, before qualifying as a school cook. While some black people in our community knew that white people didn't like them and kept themselves to themselves, my parents did the opposite. They made us get out there and become a part of the local community. They instilled in every one of us that there was nothing a white person did that we couldn't.

I learned to play the piano, the violin and the cello, and after my dad became a Methodist Lay preacher, I would play at church when the organist wasn't there. I was the first black cellist in the Nottingham Junior Youth orchestra in the late sixties.

At school I did modern ballet and outside of school on Saturdays, I learned old-time ballroom dancing. I loved the big dresses with yards of fabric and net petticoats that made them stick out. It was all about being sophisticated, possessing grace and elegance and going to dancing events and championships where black people didn't normally go. I met different kinds of people that I wouldn't usually socialise with and my confidence developed. To this day I'm not fazed by meeting new people. Ballroom linked back to my music studies because not only could I play waltzes, tangos and foxtrots on the piano, I could do the steps equally as well.

Being the only black child at school was really nice. I always felt special, and I excelled in sport, music and dance, winning medals and cups. People knew better than to even try and beat me. My younger siblings would get cross with me as I made it difficult for them to compete but they found other ways in which to excel, which put me to shame. My parents expected all of us to take opportunities.

As there were nine children in the family and three of us that were of a similar age, we were often dressed similarly and would walk down the street three abreast, all linked arms. That sort of thing was considered cute in those days. My mum was a great seamstress so we always had pretty clothes and lots of them. I used to give away my clothes to my friends and she'd be like, 'Do you know how much that cost me?! I'm not a charity!' But I had a wardrobe full of clothes and wanted to share them. I understand her reaction now.

We only faced the odd bit of racism, but when it surfaced it was horrible. I didn't know what golliwog meant, but I was hurt by the way it was said. People would lick their fingers and rub me to try and get the black off my skin. White people didn't understand Caribbean plaits, which 'stuck on your head', whereas they wore their hair in loose plaits or bunches. While they were mystified at my styles, I had hair envy.

Swimming lessons were the worst because without fail they would ask about the moisturiser we put on our skin after coming out of the swimming pool, and why the soles of our feet and the palms of our hands were lighter than our skin elsewhere. Terrible jokes would be made, but by the eighties the English finally understood the need for skin moisturiser, and by the noughties they understood that it was a necessity for men too. Game, set and match to us! Caribbeans were the trend-setters.

BOYFRIENDS AND BOARDERS

My parents were amazing people. I've spent all my life trying to be as good as they are, and when I had my own family, I tried to replicate the environment they created for me. My mum died first in 1989, aged sixty-four, and there were seventy members of the family at the funeral. By the time my dad died in 1992, at seventy-two, we didn't bother to count as there were so many of us. The children of the Windrush generation were having children and the tradition of large families was continuing.

It was gut-wrenching to have to say goodbye to them and I was particularly angry that my parents had both passed relatively young. My mum had just started to relax in life after years of hard work and helping us settle into our new home. She didn't live long enough to enjoy her retirement fully. My eldest sister who came over to be a nurse will be eighty in 2018 and will have outlived them both. Perhaps the odds are better now for Caribbeans to enjoy their retirement and reap the benefits associated with it.

One thing my parents did not approve of while we were growing up was English teenagers standing on street corners or hanging around in parks, kissing and holding hands. Such behaviour in a public place was frowned upon in the Caribbean community. All the white girls in my junior school seemed to have a boyfriend, but it was hard for me to get one where we lived because of the racism. Much to my delight in primary school, I remember a black boy came to the school and I told him, 'You're going to be my boyfriend.' I had no shame. He said, 'OK, what's the job role?' I don't suspect he quite knew what I meant and perhaps thought he had better do what he was told as he was new to the school. We're still friends to this day!

I jumped at the chance of having my first proper boyfriend when I was sixteen, but the story ends in a betrayal: mine. He was one out of half a dozen black guys in Nottingham who were doing their A levels, and every black parent held him up as a role model for their children. He was academic but humble, very 'mannersable', as we say in the Caribbean. When he was going off to university, he told his best friend, Keith, to look after me. Of course, just two months later Keith and I struck up a romantic relationship which led to us getting married some four years later. I didn't see my first boyfriend again for a long time, but when I did, he was married too and, much like with my first boyfriend, we have been friends ever since, thankfully.

I think my husband chose me because I was an ambitious girl from a nice, well-connected family. He was a year older than me and we were engaged in 1970. I left him to do the wedding formalities while I went off to university in the west Midlands. In trying to get married, they said that he wasn't entitled to be in the country because he hadn't sorted out his residency papers. He became naturalised by the time the wedding date came around, but we hadn't known the importance of those papers until then because we had all come on our parents passports as children. It was a foreshadowing of the Windrush scandal.

After we were married, in June 1972, we got a flat in a high-rise, and two years after that we got a house. We found out then that some people in our community didn't know about mortgage systems and thought they had to buy in cash, and I also learned that some Caribbeans were being refused banking services. It was then that I started taking an interest in local community work. People would come and consult me on how to access council services, improving their children's education and integrating into English culture.

However, I was feeling some pressure from the community. It felt as though I was expected to have a baby within nine months of being married and because I waited two years, people were saying that perhaps there was something wrong with me and I was infertile. The whispers really hurt. I wouldn't have minded if people had come and said it to me in a direct manner, but it was that it went on behind my back. But I was training to be a solicitor, and qualifying was my priority, not starting a family. This did not compute with some in my local community.

Ultimately I had my first child, Joanna, two years after we were married. I was young for a white person, but late for a black person. Lynda, meanwhile, was a twenty-fifth birthday present. Keith threw me a surprise party, and Lynda is the lovely result.

My children went to private school after I went to a parents' evening at our local state school for my eldest daughter only to be told she was 'average'. I was gobsmacked. I had prepared her well for school with handwriting, spelling, reading and number-work. I had built it up as a big moment which would be a glorious tale to tell my husband. I went home to him and said, 'Thank you, darling, you've let me be a stay-at-home wife, but I'm going back to work.' He said that I should let it go, but I didn't care what anyone else thought, I believed – and still believe – that my children deserve the best. And then I went back to work and sent my kids to private school. Keith feared they would lose their cultural identity in a school of that type, but I felt vindicated because boarders in that school always asked if they could come and stay at our home on weekends or school holidays. They were as keen to learn about Caribbean culture as we were delighted to share it with them through our meals, music and way of life.

I didn't quite realise how expensive it would be; instead of going on school trips to London, they went on cruises.

Britain wouldn't be where it was today without the influence and contribution of Caribbean people, but although I am proud to be a black woman, I don't think I'm in any group except the group that wants to achieve and be the best they can be. That's a group I want to be in because it's just about me, not my colour or my gender.

FRONTLINE

Paul Reid

as told to Charlie Brinkhurst-Cuff

Paul Reid is the Brixton born and bred director of the Black Cultural Archives (BCA), which is dedicated to collecting and preserving black cultural heritage. He joined the institution in 2006 to drive forward plans to give it a permanent home. Formerly Brixton Town Centre Manager for Lambeth Council, Paul has over twenty-five years' experience in community development, engagement and empowerment.

I grew up with short trousers, runny nose and a dirty neck, running up and down the streets of Brixton in south-west London. My family had a Caribbean café, and then a restaurant, on Railton Road, next door to a basement gambling house. This was at a time when it was notorious, and some of the people that were around would have had relationships with criminals like the Kray twins. It was quite tough living. I didn't get the piano lessons, the Saturday school or the Sunday school like some people did. I was probably running up and down involved in some mischievousness, trying to dodge this, that or the other.

My dad, a hardcore Jamaican who came to the UK in 1953, was highly respected in the community. He was an unsung hero in many ways because he found a way of renting a shop, one of the first of its kind, at a time when Brixton was considered by some to be a no-go zone. He would service the nightlife and people would come from all over London to eat at his table. The shop became almost like a community centre with faces coming and going.

146

Sometimes people didn't have money but if they were hungry, they would be fed. Other times, they may well have acquired *something*, and were looking to sell it.

At the basement next door, men would stack piles of money and play dice and poker at round tables, mingling with working women and pimps. Although it might sound quite seedy, these were the things that made the community gel. There were other characters like a woman called Ms Pearl, who you can't tell the history of Brixton without. She was very no nonsense; she'd knock you out if you tried to cross her. Then there was Precious, a beautiful woman. She ran a restaurant which was immediately opposite ours and was a cornerstone of the community.

My father was tall, dark and handsome. He had a lot of nice clothes and he'd mostly wear a suit and Caribbean-style hats. A gambler he may have been, but he was a beautiful man in terms of his character. When he wasn't looking, I used to try to wear his shirts, but his neck was a lot bigger than mine. He had a silent power and he wouldn't talk to you if he didn't like what you were about or what you'd just done. He wouldn't cuss you off, but you would know in his silence where you stood. In Kingston, where he was born, he would have hustled. Jamaica would've been very hard at that time, particularly in town. Unemployment levels were out the roof and elections were always linked to violence and shootings. He grew up when people were travelling around on donkeys.

Although I refer to Kingston as being home, my father's line actually came from the parish of St Mary. They were fishermen and country people. If you go back a couple of generations before, we are connected to a mythical figure in the family: an enslaved African. I sometimes sense that people think slavery was way back in the distant past. But my father had me late in life, and his father had him late in life. So you only have to step on a few stones to end up in that period.

I don't know very much about my enslaved ancestor, but I do know that some of the characteristics of my family were found within her, in terms of her absolute determination to keep going against the odds. The women in my family have a resilience of character. They held the family together while the men went mad. My ancestor would have started off low before rising – like my aunties at the market, who sat on crocus bags, selling pepper and scallion. In the course of their lives, those aunties ended up with quite a few properties and very good businesses. From humble beginnings to social and financial success.

My mum was from Liverpool, and met my dad when she moved to London and left her family behind. They were together for about nine years before they had me and she was completely embraced by my father's family. She worked for the London Underground and then Lambeth Council – something to do with lavatories. She wasn't as rebellious as my father and it was her money that regularly came in to pay the mortgage. We lived in one of those wonderful big houses in Brixton Hill, which are now crazily expensive, and had the classic front room where the children didn't go in and which was reserved for elders. If you had a house in the black community you shared it with others.

FIGHT CLUB

I learned how to cook very quickly through the takeaway and got an appreciation of money. I was tasked with counting the coppers, the 2ps and 1ps, and I hated it because I wanted to count the silvers. Over time, those coppers became my pocket money and taught me to respect the value of saving. My friends saw me as spoilt because I saved up to buy things. One time, I started skating for Streatham Redskins and bought some roller skating boots. Another time it was a bowling ball. But there was a discipline to it. I worked in the takeaway but I didn't receive proper wages. When I did once ask my dad about it I quickly found out there were no wages coming soon. My wages were called dinner.

Every morning I'd go to school early because I used to do hurdles and go to the gym before the day started. I'd come home to the shop, get dinner, and try to dive out to get into some nonsense. But I'd be put to work, and I'd often be there until quite late at night. Sometimes I used to leave the shop at 11 p.m., having worked to prepare for the night. Then I'd have to make my way from Railton Road to Brixton Hill, climb into Brockwell Park, which was all locked up, but it was the quickest way home. I used to run through the park, climb over the wall and then quickly get to my house. Looking back now, it sounds abusive, but it was great.

I went to Beaufoy School in Kennington. It was majority black boys and we were all channelled into sport; the classic case of undereducation, having to fight your way through school, and being pushed into physical exercise. At the beginning of each year I always said I was going to be really good, I was going to try my hardest. But about two weeks in, I ended up in problems. I couldn't put my finger on why it was that the intention to do well, in terms of qualifications, never materialised. Looking back, I've worked out that the environment was not conducive for learning. It was an environment that was conducive for fighting. There was a pecking order, and if you were at the top of the pecking order, then you didn't get beaten up. If you were at the bottom of the pecking order, you got beaten up, regularly. So it was important to position yourself high.

All the stuff around sport and physical prowess and, eventually, my interest in martial arts, was partly informed by having to be able to fight. I saw white boys getting beaten up regularly. Asian boys, similarly, because they were considered to be intelligent. And the rest of us got respected because of what we could do physically. That might be because you could run, were good on the rugby pitch, or could slam dunk a basketball. There was some kudos to that, and if you were intelligent, or seen in any way to have interest in education, you were picked on.

I left school in 1979, when I was sixteen. In my head I said, 'All right, everybody's gonna bounce now. And I'll go back to sixth form.' But what actually happened was, I left school on a Wednesday, walked into a place called Reed employment, found myself in an interview on the Friday, and started work on the Monday.

WE AIN'T HAVIN' IT

Growing up, I was always told that something special was going to happen in my life. On many occasions elders would say things like, 'We're gonna be dead and gone soon, and it's comin' to you.' I remember them being able to distinguish me from other children, and saying things like, 'This one's got a chance.' They had an ability to see qualities. The apologetic generation of Caribbeans gave way to the children that were born here in the 1970s and 1980s; me being one of them. We went to school here and said, 'We ain't havin' it.'

I didn't have siblings but I had what I understood as family and lots of people around me. I don't even know where half the kids came from and I'm not sure if they were my biological family. I just knew that after a certain age you called them uncle and aunty, and their children were your brothers and sisters and cousins. When I was sometimes offered money, I would be the type of child that, if I didn't feel it was right, would say, 'Thank you, uncle, but no thanks.' It was revolutionary talk because you don't turn down money as a kid. You could buy sweets! But I turned down money, and a whole range of other opportunities. I didn't necessarily know why at the time, but later on I found out that some of the characters offering it might have been unsavoury. So the money was perhaps some kind of enticement.

As far as I can go back, I remember issues of race, inequality and injustice. I was fortunate to grow up in a household where people would use moments like Muhammad Ali on TV to discuss important issues. I was soaking all of that up, and it was informing my identity, of who I am, and what needed to be done. I saw the birth of Rasta in Britain, the outpouring of anger on the streets in 1981, commonly referred to as riots, but what I refer to as uprisings because in some cases they were organised. We actually targeted authorities, and yes, some shops were broken into and things were stolen, but more importantly, pillars of the establishment in key locations were burnt down. That's more significant to me than a few leather jackets or a carriage clock. Black men especially had major conflict with the authorities, particularly the police. This is also the period of the New Cross house fire, where thirteen young black Londoners died, and the subsequent Black People's Day of Action, where hundreds of people met to discuss the failure of the government to acknowledge the tragedy.

I don't buy into the concept of 'mixed race'. Over time, the concept of race, as in species, has been discredited. There's been some very offensive language that's been created over time to describe people that have a white parent and a black parent. One of those words is *mulatto*. Another has been *half caste*. Mulatto comes from the word mule. The cross between a donkey and a horse. So, on one level, there's the fact that science has discredited the idea of race and then there's the offensive terminology. If we discredit the ideas of race, how are we buying into the concept of mixed race as a primary identity? So, I don't use it any more. I will never deny the fact that my mum is white and that she comes from Liverpool, but I'm just abandoning words that are not good for describing me even though I'm aware of the privilege I have being light-skinned.

I've gone to Jamaica, stood up in the queue at the bank, and the banker called me to the front of the queue to serve me. This was a beautiful woman, and I said to myself, 'My chances are in.' I thought she must've liked me. But, as I was trying to change my travellers' cheques, I thought it was a bit weird that the charm and charisma wasn't working and I walked away with my money. Only then to find the next time I went to the bank, a similar thing happened, and I saw an Asian man come in with a fistful of money and walk straight to the front of the queue and get served. I was very rebellious at this point in my awakening. I remember standing up in the bank, and challenging the people in the queue. 'Are you still putting up with this?' I said. 'Slavery is done.' Then I positioned myself in the line in my rightful place.

It must be recognised that some of the most horrific experiences took place in Jamaica, the most brutal of slave masters were required to handle the most rebellious of Africans. Rarely do we talk about the ongoing trauma, the echo, that has never been resolved, that still resonates within us today in our ideas around what we can and can't do – in the responses of people toward us when we try to get our confidence up and do something. This tremor is still playing out, as can be seen with the Windrush scandal.

BLACK CULTURE

After the Windrush scandal, we had to set up legal surgeries at the Black Cultural Archives. We were trying to take it to another level, because the scandal was chickens coming home to roost. We were packed, especially at the beginning. I would argue that we're all affected by the scandal. I have papers to be in this country, a birth certificate, passport, National Insurance number, everything sorted out. But there might be an uncle whose situation isn't in order, and he feels vulnerable, he's in my family, that means I'm affected. And you're a friend of mine, that means you're affected. You're concerned about the stress and the worry that I'm experiencing in relation to my uncle.

Even though the Home Office will talk about a particularly defined period of time, referred to as the Windrush generation, actually, you're talking about empire, and how at one point the British Empire, with its colonies, put an invitation out. The intelligent conversation is about the legacy of slavery, colonialism, empire. It's convenient to talk about us presently as part of the 'fabric of society', but quietly in the background be chipping away at our rights to stay. People came as British subjects, only to find a number of years later, question marks hovered above their heads as to whether or not they were British. Governments have been chipping away at our citizenship, using immigration legislation to reduce the rights of descendants. But isn't it interesting that when we were required, we were British? It's a terribly embarrassing time for the government.

It's a societal thing, and it's wrong for us to pinpoint individuals who went on holiday and couldn't get back into the country. If we just trivialise it to that example, we are forgetting that the person who went on holiday who can't get back into the country could've been living next door. Or actually, straight up and down, could've been married to your daughter. So to what extent are we really gonna take this moment to review what it is to be British, and to make the changes that are necessary?

If I'm in the face of racism and hostility, however overt or covert it may be, hell no, I do not consider myself to be British. But when I'm outside of this country, I recognise the benefits of being here. And I think that speaks to the contradiction and the tension and the discourse of what has happened. That whole fifteenth-, sixteenth-, seventeenth-century period of enslavement and colonisation. We are still seeing these issues played out, even though we went through abolition. We're still seeing and we will continue to see it as long as there is any kind of racism. Because it's the source, origin and essence that's still alive. That's why the national curriculum is mainly white and British.

After I left my first career as a vehicle buying executive, I abandoned myself. I went to a careers advice fair and met a black woman who had a photograph of Marcus Garvey hanging over her desk. She told me about him, and then when she asked what I wanted to do, I said, 'I don't want to go back to anything like where I've just been. I want to work for my community.' So we started to talk about youth and community work, without having the language for it. I had come in with a mission, but it hadn't been fully formed. She told me about going back to college as a mature student to get qualified. She was one of those black women who are almost like angels.

Eventually I went to Bulmershe College in Reading, for the most politicised youth community course in the country. As time went on, I moved on from youth and community work and eventually became the town centre manager responsible for Brixton. It was with that opportunity that I saw the building that the BCA would come to occupy. I had no money, but I saw the location, the derelict building and the BCA on Coldharbour Lane, and I started to massage the things together. But the journey from idea to the fact is trauma. There were major points where we've patted ourselves on the back for milestones achieved and how great it's been, but the development of the BCA has proved that institutional racism is alive and kicking. I'm not throwing those words out there because it almost cheapens the depths of it. Some of it is coming from the right place, and some of it is coming from hardened, stink attitudes.

One of the reasons why Black Cultural Archives has had such a difficulty in establishing itself, is because we don't have a track record in this country of building and sustaining organisations. We have a rich self-help and volunteering tradition, but black-led, black-run organisations standing on their own two feet confidently have often failed. We don't have the support we need. And although we have struggled to get government funding, in all honesty we also have to recognise that the black community are the primary stakeholders in this project, and if we can't value this history, then why should anybody else?

I don't prescribe what people are or who people are. I just believe in inviting people into opportunities to discuss and explore. There are times when black people need 'black people time' and space. We need to shut the door. We need to say some stuff to each other.

MY MONICA

Rikki Beadle-Blair

as told to Charlie Brinkhurst-Cuff

Rikki Beadle-Blair MBE is an award-winning playwright, director, actor and choreographer brought up in London by his Jamaican mother. In 1994 he wrote the screenplay for the film Stonewall, *followed by a number of screenwriting credits including the Channel 4 series* Metrosexuality. *He has written and directed plays around the experiences of the black Caribbean diaspora and the LGBT community, such as* Bashment, Shalom Baby, Familyman *and* #HashtagLightie.

I started calling my mum Monica when I heard other people addressing her by her first name. Everyone seemed to think it was amusing, but to me, as a precocious child who was close in age to her, it just seemed logical. I was born in 1961 so she was only a teenager when she became pregnant.

Monica always says that she's going to sit down with the family one day and tell us all about our Jamaican heritage, but for some reason, she doesn't. She loves Jamaica and calls it 'going home' whenever she visits, but she also has the very Jamaican attitude that you don't talk about your business to people. 'Don't shout my name out in the street, don't shout my business, don't answer the door to strangers, don't answer the door at all' was the reality of my childhood. The one way I've managed to come to understand her story is through interviewing her for the BBC. I asked her about what it was like to come to Britain.

My mum was born in Kingston. She has really happy memories from there and she spent vacations at her grandma's in the country. Her father, who I don't think she was close to at all, still lives in Kingston. She's only seen him as an adult once and I've never met him. I know she came over to the UK when she was twelve, in 1956, with her mother and her older sister. Her mother died not that long after they arrived, and when she got pregnant and decided to have a baby, that didn't go down well with her sister, who was unhappy with her for getting pregnant out of wedlock. She sat Monica down with adoption papers and told her to sign them. Instead, my mum left to live with a friend. From then on, just four years after she moved to the UK, she became clearer about her identity as a lesbian and was structuring her family independent of men – or the rest of her immediate family.

We never really had a conversation about Monica's sexuality, but it became evident to me that she was a lesbian early on in my life, because I was quite a perceptive child. Suddenly she had a partner, and we had two mums. It was always delivered to us as the most natural thing because Monica was just being herself, as opposed to explaining herself. She is a 'never apologise, never explain' kind of person. I would sometimes break things down for my younger brothers and sisters, but I never remember her explaining anything to me, just demonstrating. She had five kids in all, including my brother Gary Beadle, a successful actor.

People berate black men a lot for not sticking with their families, but my understanding of it is that once upon a time, not that long ago, they were always being ripped away from them.

That sense of security isn't there. There is a double-edged sword of young men fearing any kind of captivity, alongside a cultural DNA of 'don't get caught, don't get held down, be free because it doesn't last'. The ongoing disappointment of your family being shattered, or somebody being sent away, even your children, has made men less faithful. I do know lots of Afro-Caribbean men who are passionate about their families, but I can see that it's difficult. There isn't a heritage to monogamy.

Because of this, I do believe in the Jamaican matriarch and think Monica is one. She is a fantastic, gregarious communicator. Even though she's very private, she doesn't have any shyness. She can speak to anyone, anywhere, in any social setting. In the 2017 Grace Jones documentary, *Bloodlight and Bami*, Grace talks about how her accent changes quite dramatically depending on who she's talking to. For my mother, coming into a British school as the first black girl, like Grace, she immediately had to assimilate. If she's talking to somebody who's a Londoner, she has a very London accent, and if she's talking to somebody who's Jamaican, she has an immaculate Jamaican accent. Even if she's talking to somebody from France, she'll adopt a general European accent. But she's very much a Londoner. She lives in the city and loves it.

It's been invaluable to me as an artist, because I feel like I can talk to anybody, too. My plays speak to black audiences and mixed-raced audiences, but I can absolutely speak to Middle England. She taught me that you can be all of it, that you can have all of these different voices and never lose sight of yourself.

Nowadays she's very androgynous, like a cute little rude boy, but in the sixties she went for that very sixties look: you'd see her in slingbacks, a wig, a fitted dress, a small handbag. She looked like one of the members of singing group Martha Reeves and the Vandellas. Then in the seventies, she would burst into the room wearing big afro wigs, or she would comb her own hair out. She had 'Say It Loud – I'm Black and I'm Proud' T-shirts and bell-bottoms.

The house had all the Black Panther books, *If They Come in the Morning* by Angela Davis, *Soledad Brother* by George Jackson, *The Female Eunuch* by Germaine Greer, books by James Baldwin and gay culture dotted around, too. The music was Marvin Gaye's 'What's Going On', 'Shaft' by Isaac Hayes and Curtis Mayfield's 'Move On Up'. I was hearing black empowerment songs and could feel it in the way Monica dressed and the way she moved. She and her friends would stay up drinking and smoking until late in the night, plumes wafting around the room alongside their politics. She wasn't like one of the Shakurs of the Black Panthers, but she cared about politics and gay culture. That was really useful to me as a gay kid, because it was just part of that fabric and conversation, on the shelves and in the record collection of my home.

Because my mother was very young in the sixties and seventies, she would sometimes go to blues dances and just take me with her. No one queried why I was there and I got to see amazing things. She'll still go out raving now – I imagine mostly to lesbian places, although at Carnival she used to pull up outside of my house near

Notting Hill and then just disappear for the whole weekend. I would say, 'So where have you been?' And she'd reply, 'Oh, I've just been hanging out.' She's a survivor, so she loves to go out and dance and then sleep all day.

While I was growing up, Monica worked as a social worker, dealing with homeless young people. She would try to get them the means to move back in with their families or move into secured flats. She told me it was a problem you saw in every culture, and every class. There were more children from poor backgrounds, but she saw kids from Hampstead whose parents had kicked them out, too. Now, at seventy-four, and probably because of her line of work, she's deep into politics and will go out and knock on doors for political candidates.

LAMP POST SCHOOL

My mum taught me to write when I was three years old, and at seven I decided to be a playwright. I saw an interactive panto-mime which might've been an Anansi story, a West African and Caribbean folk tale. The idea and energy of speaking to the audience and them talking back to you had me hooked. I kept writing plays for my friends on the estate where I lived, and we would perform them in the block at the bottom of the stairs. I went to a hippy free school from the age of eleven called the Bermondsey Lamp Post, where you could learn what you liked. Led by a middle-class woman named Lois Acton (who remains a dear friend and member of my family), it had no money and gave you no qualifications, but it was one of the most crucial things that happened to me in my childhood, besides learning to read so early.

The school totally transformed my life and it continues to inspire and ground me in everything I do to this day. They supported kids who weren't attending the local comprehensives, especially those from broken homes. In a 1973 BBC *Nationwide* documentary made about the school, you can see me directing one of my plays – a production of *Robin Hood*. I was bold and confident in my skills as a playwright even from that age. The school gave me the freedom to write, direct, produce and design all on my own, unlike the comprehensive I went to for Year 7, where I was made fun of for having a big afro, being gay and being intelligent.

Growing up, we moved around bedsits in Peckham, Camberwell and Bermondsey. There were some terrible experiences, with exploitative landlords putting up rents fast and trying to sexually assault Monica. Sometimes we had to leave in the middle of the night with nowhere to go. She had a tough time because she had a family but no partner, so she was considered to be sexually experienced and available. In the sixties, women weren't even allowed to have their own bank accounts. As her burgeoning lesbian identity became more apparent people would react badly to that as well. She had to fight her way through the council system to get us accommodation. She would diligently go to the council every day until she secured something.

Despite being ripe for exploitation and disrespect, Monica was always teaching us to respect ourselves and not be defined by the things that were happening to us. South-east London was tough and we were brought up in an environment where it was an achievement if none of your children went to prison and none of us ever have. The BNP, which was founded in 1982, were on the march and people would spit in my face in the street. You had to get minicabs because taxis wouldn't stop for you. Before attending Lamp Post, I went to Dog Kennel Hill School, at the top of a hill in East Dulwich. All the rich kids came from big houses on the Camberwell side, while on the other side there were council estates. One of my best friends, Sean, was from a very poor family who was barely surviving, using scraps for curtains – I remember their house smelled bad – but he was very bright, open and creative. When I used to go around there, his parents would say, 'I'm not letting a *nigger* in my house,' and he would be humiliated because he wanted me to come in and play.

Then you'd go to the rich side of the hill, and the parents would let you in the house, but then they'd say things like, 'You speak English very well, Rikki.' I'd go, 'Yeah, I am English.' After a while I realised that to them I wasn't; it didn't matter that I was born here at the same time, possibly in the same hospital, as their child. Even with my friends, we might get into an argument, and suddenly I would be a nigger.

I saw these microaggressions and full-frontal aggressions all at the same time, all the while saying, 'I want to be a writer, I want

166

to be a director.' There were no black writers, no black-British writers, no black-British directors. It was hard.

On the flipside, going to the black barbers was always kind of scary. It was one of the places where I started to realise that certain people think that there are parameters you have to fit to be black. People would often say to me in the barbers, 'So what music you listen to?' as if to say 'How black are you?' I was listening to Isaac Hayes and Philly soul, but I was also listening to David Bowie and glam rock. There was a sense of embracing your culture, but also thinking – will they accept me? Am I allowed to have this accent? Am I allowed to read all these books? Because in working-class and black culture there's sometimes a suspicion of academia.

What I learned from my mother was that I don't have to make myself black. She taught me, just by the way she held herself and the things she would say, that there's no speed limit for how you should live your life and this isn't a motorway. You don't have to stay in your lane. You can cross lanes, you can leave and come back on, you can go off a split road, you can take your own path. You can have your own mix of friends; you can have your own mix of cultures. Black is a lot of different things.

I don't sleep much at all and I don't drink or take drugs. I'm all about the work. Typing, designing, making music late into the night I'll ask myself, 'How can we conquer the world and change it today?' That's what my drive is. I just pathologically create. The ultimate piece I really want to do is a great modern musical that uses all the influences I have: from soul and reggae and hip-hop to rock and classical and indie. It would be a monolithic legacy piece, like my own *West Side Story*.

WRESTLING EMPIRE

I think a lot about having a slave-owner's name because my ancestry stops with a particular plantation. I didn't meet my grandparents but I spent a lot of time with my great-aunt, who lived to 101. She was born before there were planes in the sky or many cars on the road and was middle-aged when radio and TV came on. I'm fascinated by the extraordinarily quiet life she had as a child where there was no noise. She cooked everything she ate and never had a McDonald's in her life. She went to hospital twice; once when she was seven and once to die. She lived across the road from my family so my mum could look after her right till the end.

What upset me the most about the Windrush scandal was the fact that they did it to old people who struggled for such a long time. If my great-aunt was still alive, it could have affected even her – someone who was so hard-working, so law-abiding, who had followed all the rules. She went to church every Sunday, never made a noise, never demanded anything, never complained, never said, 'Where are my reparations?' Never talked about the anger of slavery. She was somebody who tried to do good, be quiet, and *be*. It's people like her that they went after.

You try and live a life that's full of love, but the scandal makes it almost impossible to not feel a surge of anger. It's hard not to see it as racialised because they weren't shipping white people back to Australia. If you've got eyes, you can see who's being deported and who's being focused on. Just like Trump never talks about white immigrants, he talks about Mexican immigrants. He's talking about the 'browning of America'.

For me, there would be challenges with living in Jamaica. As a gay man, I'm aware that it's not always a welcoming place. I worked on a documentary for Radio 4 in 2001 about homophobia in Ragga music, which inspired my 2005 play *Bashment*. I found the LGBT community in Jamaica very interesting. What you saw was exactly what you get everywhere. Young people were hanging out in the street, being loud, voguing. I was a little confused because I thought it would be too dangerous for them to be out in the open like that, but I remember stopping by the side of the road and suddenly there was a whole gaggle of gay kids there coming out of a club. They were going, 'Hello darling! Your boyfriend's nice!' So, it's not as cut and dry and depressing as you think.

At the same time, they also told me horrendous stories of neighbours turning on people and chopping them up, chasing them to the church to kill them, and the murder of activists. The activists out there are trying to lobby parliament to try and make laws to reduce the violence, but we must remember that it is archaic British buggery laws that were put in place during empire that influenced the current homophobia we see in the country – the same laws that imprisoned Oscar Wilde. Homosexual sex is still illegal in Jamaica under sections 76 and 77 of the 1861 Offences Against the Person Act.

Monica didn't go to Jamaica at all during my childhood as we didn't have the money to travel, but she happened to be in the country during the recording of the documentary. I said to her, 'How can you feel at home here when it's so homophobic?' She said that the killings were rare and that you just get on with your life. 'People know uncle in this village is gay,' she said as an example. 'We all know about him and no one talks about it. I think people get upset here when you talk about it.' Of course, being younger than her, I think it's our right to be able to talk about it openly. But that's how things are in Jamaica.

It all reflects back on imperialism. The colonists shamed African people for their 'nakedness', for their godlessness and for their sensuality. We absorbed our lessons and became these god-fearing Christians who were more Christian than our oppressors, to prove to them that we were not subhuman heathens. Now, we're still wrestling with the beauty of that: the beauty of music, worship, ritual and the oppressiveness of that imposition. We turn it on each other. You get education, expansion, repression and contradiction all at the same time. There's the homophobia and harsh punishments for kids. As people of colour in this culture and in the world, we have to learn how to strike a balance between all of it. Between what we've been, what's been taken away, what we've been given, what we've learned and what we're having to reclaim.

Empire is complicated. It's cruelty, slavery, exploitation,

savagery and limitation, but I wouldn't be here without it, and I do like being here at this incredible time. I don't like the kind of cultural struggle that Britain is in, but I love the fruits of it; the posh kids you hear walking around Camden and Hampstead using black slang, trying to talk like Dizzee Rascal; straight kids going to Pride, and using lots of gay slang like 'slay' and 'queen', and 'I'm living for this'. It goes back and it comes forward until you don't know where anything began or started and the Empire is part of that.

I was very ambivalent about whether I wanted to accept my MBE – which is an Order of the British Empire – in 2017. I have friends who have said no to it and I understand that. But for me, I thought it would be great for kids of all races to see that you can be a member of British society. They're not on the outside, the down low, or the margins. We are a part of this fabric of what built this country and what it will become.

It's inspiring to go to a majority black country like Jamaica. But actually I like being in a country where it's really mixed. If you go to somewhere like Italy there's amazing culture, amazing food, amazing people, amazing fashion. But they all look the same. But then you get off in London, and accents are like a geography lesson as you walk down the street. I don't want to live somewhere where everybody looks the same. But I understand that we're all brainwashed in different ways.

CARIBBEAN BODIES, NORTHERN SOUL

Kemi Alemoru

Kemi Alemoru is a 24-year-old journalist working for Dazed *and* gal-dem. *She is based in London, but was born in Manchester, to a dual-heritage Jamaican and Nigerian family. Much of her career has seen her cast a critical eye on pop culture, politics and identity to unpick how they all intertwine.*

The way we think of England is generally London plus everything else. When it comes to black British history, which is already dismally taught, most of it focuses on the struggles and spectacles of those who settled in the capital. Brixton, Notting Hill and Peckham are often namechecked as West Indian hotspots, particularly for the first arrivals, yet we rarely hear of the experiences of Bradford's West Bowling Caribbeans, or those who flocked to industrial regions like Coventry. The few times we hear about racial tension and uprisings it's the Brixton riots in the eighties that gets a mention way before Toxteth in the same year, or Nottingham's in 1958. These narratives differ, and they matter just as much. So, in the absence of a decent black British history curriculum in UK schools, it's up to oral history to commemorate these experiences.

Anyone who has visited Manchester over the last decade can testify that there is near-constant redevelopment in the regions around the city centre. Barely anything ever looks the same from one visit to the next. This, paired with an increasingly ageing Windrush generation, means that soon the landmarks that were once core to the Caribbean community may not only disappear but be completely forgotten. As a third-generation Nigerian-Jamaican-Mancunian born in the nineties, there are decades of stories that I rarely think to ask about. In recent years I've become far more inquisitive because all I've ever known is England and parents who are basically English. It was never a struggle for me to navigate white spaces given that I encountered them more than black ones. I wanted to find out more about where Caribbeans went to maintain a sense of community, and knew I needed some guides who had seen the streets change.

My maternal grandparents, who are now edging closer to ninety, are named Gretel and David Bell. Since my mother was born they have always lived in Old Trafford, not very far away from the cricket ground, hence why I called my maternal grandmother 'Grandma Trafford' until alarmingly recently. I meet them on a Saturday evening, as they recline on their dark leather sofas surrounded by framed pictures of me and my cousins and old Mother's and Father's Day cards. Silver braids frame Grandma's face, and her eyes are near-closed. Grandad has a tray on his lap. I've made a habit of dropping in on them just to listen to them speak. Both are full from a dinner of chicken with rice and peas, a simple dish they missed upon arrival in the UK.

'I could not eat the meat. It never had any taste,' my grandma tells me with a frown on her face. 'It took me ages before I could eat it. And, it was also here that I came to eat spud – we never ate spud at home. If we had them we would maybe put one in a soup but that was it. Yet, when I came here it became my main meal. We weren't used to it.' This revelation, although small, illustrated how many things go unsaid because they seem inconsequential. They actually reveal the everyday reality of relocating, and integrating.

My grandma arrived in England in January 1961, after her older sister who lived in Birmingham sent for her. She landed in London and, as first impressions go, she wasn't best pleased. 'Everywhere looked like a factory, like it had no homes, because all the houses have chimneys on top,' she laughs. 'In Birmingham my first job was at Edgbaston School of Science; I was the assistant cook. One of the times the main cook was making a stew in a big industrial pot because there were a lot of mouths to feed. She took it out to stir it and everything turned over onto the floor and she just scraped it all up. When the dinner was finished everybody brought their plates. She realised one of the workers upstairs didn't get any dinner so she collected all the scraps onto one plate and put it in a ting to hot it up and gave it to me to carry up. Yet they didn't think much of our cooking.'

As Grandma was settling into unfamiliar territory, my grandad had already been in England since 1955, having arrived on a boat named the *Auriga*. He first settled in London, living in a house in Brixton while he worked in construction before going to Birmingham, where the pair first met. They had seen each other back home in Croft's Hill, Clarendon, but he was mostly interested in looking after his cows. My grandma, on the other hand, loved going dancing in the dresses her sister sent back home from England. As fate would have it my grandparents ended up living in the same house-share in Birmingham, before moving to Manchester where they eventually married. 'We needed a house, because we lived in one room. All of us. Me, your grandad, and three children. It was hard,' Grandma recalls. 'We tried to get a house in Birmingham but we couldn't. The people there were so racist. There was always something wrong why they wouldn't let us have it. David knew a man in Manchester – someone he called his cousin – he helped us find this house here.'

FINDING A HOME AWAY FROM HOME

For the first generation of Caribbean expats in Manchester, the home was the focal point, not just for family life but also for nightlife, due to the hostile atmosphere of some of the bars in the city. It was where they felt most comfortable. 'Everybody knew each other. They used to have a lot of house parties, down the cellar and have people round in the front room,' says Grandad. 'We were happy.'

The front room was a space that was used to entertain guests. Recently, Michael McMillan penned an entire book revisiting the distinctive decor to highlight how central it was to British-Caribbean life.' With time, the gaudy patterned walls in my grandparents' home have been painted over with a muted cream shade, and the carpets have been replaced. However, there's still a drinks cabinet and trolley which my mum, Joanne, says used to have shot glasses and cakes on when friends were in the house. As my grandparents watched the six o'clock news when I sat with them after school I'd go in search of those dark rum cakes and try to take inconspicuous slices. With their drinking days behind them there was always a bottle of Shloer nearby.

Then there's the cabinet that always perplexed me – the one full of pastel-coloured china plates and cups that were barely ever touched and used as a 'showpiece', only eaten off when you had special visitors. Grandma says it was easier congregating in other Caribbean homes because in those days the white people would 'colour bar'. 'They didn't want you. So us blacks we had to accommodate ourselves.' Each front room was therefore equipped with a radiogram to listen to the popular music of the day. Grandad smiles as he remembers how they'd play 'all sorts of records – Jim Reeves, Fats Domino, Elvis Presley dem'.

My grandparents put their partying days behind them when Grandma was approached by some Christian women in the local 'wash house'. Recently she celebrated fifty years of becoming a Christian and going to the New Testament Church of God, which lies a stone's throw away from the Whalley Pub, another

---

* McMillan, Michael, *The Front Room: Migrant Aesthetics in the Home*, Black Dog Publishing, 2009

community hub which has recently been turned into flats. 'My life changed. I came into a new life and I found it to be sociable and enjoyable when I went to church,' she says.

There's nothing particularly remarkable about a church being a community hub, but the manner in which this church was founded showed how Caribbeans felt it was vital to have their own space in the city. Unwelcome in other local churches, they pooled their resources and bought the building when it was broken down and rebuilt it together.

Every Sunday, pristinely dressed women with extravagant hats would arrive with their suited and booted husbands to sing for hours. A chorus of 'hallelujah' and 'praise him' in an island twang always filled the air as children – including me – would bang tambourines or natter at the back of the hall. There were periods of time where there would be one or two white faces, but on the whole this church was a sea of blackness. I spent alternate Sundays at this church, listening out for the chords on the piano that signified that children's church was starting and I'd be led to upstairs classes to sing and read. It's the kind of place where if you wanted to dance down the aisles it wouldn't be at all uncouth, in fact it was always actively encouraged.

Some people find believing in God laughable or think it's cringeworthy or vague if you describe yourself as 'spiritual'. My upbringing meant I find it completely tangible seeing the joy it brought into the lives of those around me.

With its sense of community and trust, the church became a reliable place to find a 'pardner' (sometimes spelt *paadna* or *pardna*) scheme. As the community found it difficult to acquire bank loans they formed saving and loans system in which they would contribute a regular sum weekly and then every week someone would get the draw, or they could request their draw early in case of emergencies. 'If you want to purchase something you'd throw in your hand [a contribution of up to £20]. My first pardner money was used to pay my mortgage and pay my tax. This house was £2,500. People still do that now,' Grandma explains. But you should only enter into it with people you trust. 'No one has ever run off with the money and some of them go up to £2,000.' With each house purchased, mortgage paid, or car bought, the congregation put down their roots.

Even though it provided them with a strong social circle, not everybody was into the frequent church trips. 'Oh my God, I hated it,' my mum laughs, although she's quite religious now. 'After a while we were going every Monday, Tuesday, Wednesday, Thursday – don't ask me why but we were going. When I was fifteen I thought, "Right, I'm going to rebel."'

Mum met her first boyfriend and started to take more of an interest in the city's nightlife. As she tells me about her experiences, I suddenly feel as though my partying days were a rehash of the decades that preceded – electronic music in Sankeys reminiscent of the long hours she spent on Wigan Pier, nights dressed up in late noughties ensembles, dancing and sweating in Factory, the club that now stands where the Factory Records offices were, years after the record label boss Tony Wilson had died. The Manchester my mum navigated with her first boyfriend was more vibrant, more original. I'm envious. 'He'd always take me into town or to all-dayers, everywhere,' she continues. 'But he would never go to Moss Side.'

MOSS SIDE STORY

Unlike my grandparents, a large amount of Windrush settlers found cheap housing in nearby Moss Side. I've fond memories of the area given that my primary school was on the edge of it. I learned to swim in its leisure centre, and I played out on the streets outside rows of red brick terraces with my childhood best friend – until we got so hungry we'd go and buy patties from Alvino's bakery with our pocket money. However, during the sixties and seventies, Moss Side became the epicentre of a slum clearance scheme that saw the council demolish countless Victorian houses that the area's former Conservative MP, James Watts, described as 'unfit for human habitation'. I'd always heard how the area was once highly regarded, with rows of shops that sold everything from jewellery to furniture. My grandparents walked me round the house and pointed to the items they'd acquired from Alexandra Road, which was frequently referred to by locals as 'Alec Road'. A fridge, a wardrobe, cabinets – they said it was like going into town and 'the blacks used to shop there because it had everything you would need'.

My mother has fond memories of day trips to the then well-kept Alexandra Park where she would eat sandwiches and look at the boats. I can't recall seeing boats there in my lifetime. Everyone in my family that I spoke to seemed to agree that knocking down the houses set off a chain of events that started to ruin the reputation of the area, and due to the fact it was the hub for Manchester's Afro-Caribbeans there is an understandable paranoia.

'It feels like a conspiracy that I'll never be able to make sense of. When I look back, all of these people would have had beautiful old houses and what they did was turn it into a slum which then had gang warfare. They created a ghetto. I'll always have a question mark as to why,' says my mother. Large houses similar to those in the now extremely trendy Chorlton area made way for rows of new houses on a controversial, tightly packed estate, and in the process many families were displaced to other areas like Cheetham Hill.

Prominent figures like community leader Professor Gus John described the devastation to the BBC in 2017. 'The houses were very sturdily built and could have been renovated with some help from government . . . the area could have been spruced up. What they were doing was not just demolishing old houses, they were demolishing communities – there never was that sense of integrated community identity [again].'

Matters were made worse in 1981 when the area was affected by riots. I'd heard – through my mother, not from any formal education – that Brixton and Toxteth had already seen uprisings that year and, with the same patterns of unemployment and police brutality, the frustration spread to Manchester. In 2006, Elouise Edwards, who worked as a community development worker, told the *Manchester Evening News* that she 'could see and hear police driving up and down Moss Lane East, beating their armour, shouting, "Nigger, nigger, nigger, oi, oi, oi," and chasing the kids all over', while Gus John, another witness, said he saw numerous youngsters assaulted with batons.

My aunty Sharon, just nineteen at the time, stood and watched the carnage from Princess Road, near where the riots broke out. 'I was in college and we just heard a whispering and everyone said, "There's going to be trouble on Princess Road, everybody get down there", she says. 'Remember, I'm not from Moss Side, I'm from Old Trafford. We just went to go and have a look. We were being faas [nosey]'.

However, youthful curiosity soon turned to terror once they witnessed the extent of the damage. 'When we got down there all we saw was people looting, one shop was actually burning. I saw young people taking furniture and also people I knew weren't from the area. We were told there were people from Salford who had come down to help make trouble.' That's to say that just like the 2011 Manchester riots there were white people there from other areas that didn't suffer the same level of vilification. Eventually, police vans came and my aunty says she didn't want to get caught up in the drama. 'Our parents didn't even know that we were down there', she adds.

In the years that followed, the area's name would become synonymous with crime and violence. In 1994, the year I was born, there were reports that Moss Side was one of the most deprived areas in Britain. The *Independent* noted that there had been about

400 armed incidents in a year in the area. While bands like the Happy Mondays and Stone Roses made waves nationwide, the Madchester craze that birthed the legendary Haçienda nightclub put the city on the map. All of the above fuelled the narcotics trade and gang crime in areas like Moss Side and Cheetham Hill and earned the city the nickname 'Gunchester'.

Still, Sharon feels the denigration of the area has been unfair. 'I used to live in Moss Side and it was fine. The only thing I didn't like is that everybody knows your business because they all sit out in front of the houses in the summertime, since they have no gardens. They were just watching people, seeing who came in and out of your house. It was still a community. White people were scared of going through it but I just have to laugh because look at Wythenshawe.' As the Wythenshawe region was the filming location for Channel 4's gritty comedy *Shameless*, I'd have to agree.

SUB-CULTURES AND CLUB CLIQUES

In all of the years I spent reassuring white friends that they wouldn't actually get shot if they walked through Moss Side, I hadn't ever realised that the media's portrayal of the area actually erased decades of community history. Particularly, its vibrant club culture. Nightlife in Manchester was always an avenue to explore identity. When the first generation ventured from their front rooms, they could seek solace in the multicultural hub that had more relaxed door policies. Bars were dotted along Denmark Road, on the border of the neighbouring Hulme area. Clubs like the Nile would cater to black people and play songs they knew from back home and curious white people would join them and discover new cultures.

'There were some Irish people,' Grandad says. 'But I didn't go out with the Irish much because as soon as they have dem drink they fight everybody.' Although in his day integration was rare, Mum recalls how Manchester's nightlife demographic began splitting along the lines of genre rather than heritage. She went to parties from lunch to midnight all the way on Wigan Pier where a mixed crowd bodypopped to electro, funk and Northern Soul – the latter genre would spin from the decks of Placemate 7 and Legends on Whitworth Street as DJs hunted for rare black American records. The venue was formerly known as the Twisted Wheel, a place often cited as being one of the birthplaces for the Northern Soul scene.

However, for black patrons looking for reggae and soul, a club named PSV in Moss Side was the place to be on a Friday. By the time she became a regular to PSV my mum had another boyfriend. 'Your dad used to put on requests for me and the DJ would say, "This one goes out to Joanne." It was so cheesy but we had a really good time,' she explains.

It was only when I started telling people my background when I moved to London that I was made aware my heritage was unique. I've been told that my ethnic mix makes me a unicorn. 'Even in the eighties, Nigerians rarely mixed with Caribbeans. Your dad told me he was half-Jamaican, half-African. He denies that until this day but he definitely did,' my mum says. At least some places were more mixed than others, like the Reno basement club underneath the Nile, which my mum dubbed 'the centre of the mixed-race revolution'. It closed and was knocked down in 1986, but it was so pivotal in a woman named Linda Brogan's life that recently she led a campaign to excavate the site.

'In my opinion, the majority of people who went to the Reno in its heyday 1972 to 1981 were mixed race. We congregated in the same place – a bit like the Italians in the film *Goodfellas*,' the Jamaican-Irish playwright Brogan tells me. 'If you were mixed race or "half-caste", as we were known then, you were "made" in the Reno. And a lot of us were born or brought up in Moss Side, conceived in the times of "No blacks, no Irish, no dogs".'

Loved by Mancunian nightlife icons like the aforementioned Tony Wilson of Factory Records fame, who had his stag night there, and snooker player Alex 'Hurricane' Higgins, soon other celebrities paid visits to the hedonistic club, including Muhammad Ali. It's even rumoured that Bob Marley was once in attendance.

Now, Brogan has dug up a hidden part of Manchester's history with a team of volunteers who were once patrons of the club. According to a recent *Guardian* article, she unearthed the basement venue that lay just beyond Hulme's historic brewery and found record shop bags, flares, bottles, marijuana and more on the site. 'I didn't excavate the Reno with the intention to make people know the Reno existed,' she explains. 'The roots of the project began in me wanting to assert my identity as mixed race. As I was pissed off with the world saying I was black. Which excludes my mum from the equation and she was my predominant carer. The one place that my identity as mixed race was valued and a badge of honour was the Reno. I went back there to find the true me.'

Moss Side still hosts an annual reminder of the Caribbean community's presence in Manchester, as Alexandra Park remains the site for the Caribbean Carnival. Even though that comes with its own struggles. Having switched hands from a community group from St Kitts and Nevis to Manchester city council a few years back, there are relatives and residents with complaints that it is morphing into a music festival rather than an artistic celebration of identity. Still, I'll keep attending to enjoy one of the few landmarks left in the area that honours the rich contributions West Indians made to the city. My aunty told me she still drives past the site where old community centres like Gus John's 8411 youth club used to exist just to reminisce, while Mum laughs as she remembers all the places, sights and sounds she never stopped to realise had gone.

Hopefully, in the face of the city's regeneration, the influence of Manchester's Windrush citizens can not only be preserved but deservedly publicised. With each visit home I learn something new about my hometown, which is testament to the fact that even the most ordinary of places can hold extraordinary meanings to some, even if they never stopped to think about it.

MY FATHER'S HANDS

Kay Montano

as told to Charlie Brinkhurst-Cuff

---

*Kay Montano is a make-up artist and story-seeker from west
London with roots in Trinidad. She has worked all over the
world with photographers such as Helmut Newton, Steven
Meisel, Bruce Weber and Mario Testino, and runs the media
platform* ThandieandKay *alongside her best friend Thandie
Newton.*

'I fell in love with his hands, dear,' is what my mother used to say about my father.

My mother was an eccentric public school girl from Somerset, and when she met my father she was already engaged to somebody else. They were at a Communist meeting which my father attended because he was a journalist and my mother went to because she was curious and unusual. My father had the skin-tone and frame of Barack Obama, though less handsome. If he'd arrived in London forty years later, he would have been a real mover and shaker.

When I got older, I would ask my mother for all the details of their relationship because there were so few black people around. 'But how?' I would say. 'He was a black guy, were you aware that your relationship would be perceived as weird? Did people stare? What did you think when you saw a black man? Wasn't that strange for you, especially coming from the country?' Most Londoners would never have seen a black person, and my mum was from Somerset. But she just didn't acknowledge those details.

My father came to England at a time when very few West Indians were here, just before *Windrush*, to work for the *Trinidadian Chronicle* on British news. You can imagine what a special position it was, how hard he must've had to work to earn it and how very well educated, ambitious and hardworking he must have been to have got to a point where they were going to pay for him to travel. After his stint with the *Chronicle*, he worked for the BBC World Service, likely researching, and by the end of his life he was a civil servant.

London was a small place back then and if you were black and a journalist, you would've known everyone who was exciting. When I was fourteen and playing a hip-hop record which sampled Malcolm X, my mother said, 'Oh, your father met him, dear!' and I know that two of my father's friends were West Indian royalty, the kings of the Windrush generation. The first was Jan Carew, a highly respected academic on colonialism, who was an extraordinary painter. The other was Learie Constantine, my parents' best man, who was a famous cricketer. He was such a wonderful figure; he fought in World War Two for the British, and he also ended up becoming a politician.

My parents were married in 1958 and they didn't actually want children, but I came along as a bit of an accident ten years into their marriage. She was forty-one and he was fifty. He never got the chance to parent me but I think he would've been a strict father and probably quite hardcore in terms of pushing my intellectual ability. He would've subscribed to that old-fashioned West Indian ideology of parents deciding what their children are going to be. They thought you were just like plasticine, and you could be moulded into a doctor or a lawyer. I don't know if that would've been great for me, because I'm not very good with authority. When people try and control me, I rebel.

My mother did most of the parenting because my father was at work. The only traditional thing about my family was the fact that every day he went out to work at City Hall, and I was in bed by the time he got home at 7.30 p.m. They divorced when I was eight and he became a Saturday father. He'd buy me things, and not say much. He was a bit rubbish, really. But it was a different time. Dads weren't brought up to be all touchy feely with children. Children were seen and not heard. I don't think he thought that there was anything going on inside my head. He didn't think that he could talk to me. Looking back, I have a feeling that he was not a happy man. I sense his unfulfillment.

My father passed away when I was nine, after he had a second heart attack. He wasn't taking his medication, and I think my mother – being an ex-nurse – should've been more responsible with him. Even though they were divorced, she could've just said, 'Well tough titty, you've got a kid. You should be alive, so just take your medication, I don't care that it makes you groggy.' But he had very high blood pressure and he didn't take his medicine, so he died.

GROWING UP WINDRUSH

My mother was bipolar so my childhood was pretty nuts after his death. That's another reason why I'm not exactly happy-clappy when it comes to investigating my past beyond the therapy I've had to navigate it healthily. It's a 'pick your battles' deal.

She was very unconventional, so when I was in my teenage rebellious phase and I'd go out to clubs, she'd be like, 'Oh, that's a nice outfit.' And when I wanted to dye my hair pink when I was fourteen, she said, 'Oh, it's a pretty colour!' She saw everything for what it was, rather than what people or society thought. That was what was brilliant about her. Emotionally, of course, she was often not at all present. Both of my parents had bad tempers and I grew up in a very volatile household, with them reactively arguing and shouting. I was relieved when they divorced because I couldn't bear the sound of them arguing as I went to sleep.

After my father died my mother had a breakdown and was admitted to hospital. I went to live with a Jamaican family who were good friends with my father. I went from being quite a twee student at John Betts primary school, where I was the darkest one in the class, believe it or not, to being on a council estate living with Jamaicans for two and a half months, eating rice and peas. Thinking back, where I grew up was all Windrush. My area, between Chiswick and Shepherd's Bush, was a great mix of Irish, middle-class white people, black people and West Indians.

Being a light-skinned mixed-race person, when I was around black people, I was considered white, and when I was around white people, I'd be dark. Even so, my experience of racism has been more second-hand. I always say to people that I have beige privilege because people don't always assume I have black ancestry. Rather than that making me feel like I didn't fit in, which I didn't really, it made me learn to interpret a different type of liberated identity. I remember at school my Caribbean peers used to shout 'tar baby' out of the window at the African kids and that's when, deep down, I started cultivating my understanding of colourism and racism. I know that white people are the worst perpetrators of it, but unfortunately that sense of shame carries itself onto and into our culture. So whatever gets you to liberation is a good thing; whether that means identifying with being white, identifying with being black, or identifying with being mixed and still identifying as black. It's not for anyone to ever dictate.

The difference between my generation and first-generation Caribbeans was that they really tried to assimilate. Every Sunday they'd be off to church wearing white crochet hats, and their white tights, and their lacy white dresses. And then because of the backlash my generation received we thought, 'You don't want me here, you don't like me, you're racist, and I'm gonna get into black consciousness.'

I had a really varied upbringing. I know what it was like growing up in England, and what London was like through the seventies and eighties. The flavour of it, and how it all felt, what it looked like, what we were listening to, and the sus laws [the police's stop and search policy] at the time. My memories of the 'Black is Beautiful' movement play through my mind like the most stylish film ever. It was so visually rich with an incredible soundtrack. The way the black girls dressed was the coolest – with such attitude. They would walk just *so* and no one would ever be in a hurry, always chill. They'd have an afro comb in their hair, just perched in there for when they might have to just comb it out. All the girls were wearing vests and long A-line skirts and flip-flops. 'Police and Thieves' was the song, and Althea and Donna – Lovers Rock. Janet Kay ('Silly Games') was the queen.

The Jamaican family I used to stay with taught me a lot and my memories of that time are almost photographic. I can see them and I can still taste that chicken and rice, the way their mother would always put tomatoes on the side and how everyone put tabasco on their chips – a brilliant mix of British and Jamaican. The kids were called Karleen and Kenrick. Karleen was fourteen when I was nine and Kenrick was fifteen or sixteen. He became a bit of a 'bad boy'. I saw him going from a nice little thing with his 'proper' combed hair, to growing his dreadlocks and putting incense all over the house, smoking weed amidst a backdrop of heavy, heavy Dub. It was the first dramatisation of Jamaican life for me, similar in comedy to the world depicted in Zadie Smith's *White Teeth*, or *East is East*. A lot of it makes me laugh so much. I can remember the dynamic of Kenrick wanting to start locking up his hair. It would drive his mother mad. 'Kenrick! Stop locking up your hair! Why you nuh comb ya hair?!' It upset them so much, because the first generation behaved.

This strange, bonkers environment was completely different to my home life. Because I was only nine, I felt a little bit unprotected. Karleen, five years my senior, would drag me off to places like Brixton, saying, 'Oh the movie *Grease* is only on there,' and I was so naïve that I didn't realise that she was lying, and wanted to go down there because it was the cool edgy place to visit and she fancied some boys. Teenagers wanted to go where the danger was and Shepherd's Bush wasn't 'The Frontline', as part of Brixton was named. My memories are of being dragged around by Karleen to shebeens where boys used to ask girls to grind against the wall. It was outrageous and I remember the thick smell of marijuana and incense: the heavy dub and the sound systems. And then Kenrick coming in from nights out after escaping through the window.

MAKING IT UP

After leaving Karleen and Kendrick's, I lived with my mother up until I was eighteen, but I was working as a make-up artist from sixteen. Coming from west London, I always knew I wanted to be a creative in the sense that I loved music, fashion and style.

When people think of west London now they think of Notting Hill, hedge funders, Chelsea. But Chelsea used to be rough and ready – artistic and affordable. As a mixed-race young person I was in my element because of my anti-authoritarian ways and being allowed to be quite free, by my eccentric, unique mother. There was plenty of trauma in my childhood but artistically, I had incredible, rich experiences.

By the time I was sixteen, I'd been clubbing seriously for two years. It was about music, the amazing parties, and the brilliant nightlife, as opposed to how we might have felt inwardly with pills. I met a pop star through the clubs and she said, 'What do you want to do?' and I said I wanted to be a make-up artist. She was in a band called Haysi Fantayzee, which was massive in the eighties. She was wild-looking and used to wear spray-painted corsets and lived in a warehouse before they were cool.

I had bleach-blonde dreadlocks and you know it takes years to grow dreadlocks, fuck's sake, so I cut some of it short. I looked tragic. Like a complete freak with so much make-up on. But the lovely thing was that I felt absolutely no societal or peer pressure to dress sexily. Whatever tribe you were from, girls didn't dress sexy – or if they did, it was in a non-submissive-looking way, in a rubber dress with spiky hair and bitchy-looking make-up. The only girls that dressed sexy were naff, tarty girls. I know it's perceived very differently now in the Kardashian era, as it's all about self-care, and 'I'm loving myself'. But, hoiking your tits out with padded enhancement feels a little regressive to my generation, even though we never perceived nudity per se in simple, sexualised terms. All the girls in clubs when we were young wore leggings and big Buffalo bomber jackets, polo necks, and flat shoes or massive DMs.

So what was it like being a make-up artist? It was amazing, and I loved that it was all about cross-cultural references. The fashion business in the eighties was full of gay people and there would frequently be black models, and models with albinism. The subculture I specifically used to work with was called Buffalo, which was a name taken from a Caribbean expression used to describe rude boys and rebels. It was led by an amazing stylist called Ray Petri, who was one of the first people to use Naomi Campbell and lots of beautiful black men. It was quite political to put a black guy in a cowboy hat back then, but Ray would always do it and make them look alpha male. Black culture has always heavily influenced London and they all used to listen to reggae. Everything that was and is cool is always connected to black culture.

In terms of the make-up itself, I was wearing the wrong colour eighties powdery foundation, as was everyone else. Even the gorgeous singer Sade has got the completely wrong colour on, if you look back at pictures. Strangely enough the iconic Shu Uemura brand, which was withdrawn in 2017 by L'Oréal, was the first place that I went to that actually had my olive skin tone. Then MAC and Bobbi Brown came out. But it was really hard at first, and I did struggle when I was working with black girls. I would go to stage make-up shops because you could rely on them to get certain colours. Not from a department store, forget about it. I'd mix them together, but it was always a bit of an issue if I had someone particularly dark.

The best part about my job is the extraordinary people I've met and the extraordinary situations I've been in rather than the work itself. I don't mean to sound ungrateful, but I mastered make-up by the time I was eighteen or nineteen so it doesn't mean much to me anymore. Now I'm in my fifties, it's something I can do with my eyes closed. I honour my input in the sense I've worked really hard and I know I'm really good at it. It's just that deep down I'm probably more of a truth-seeker than a myth-maker, like my journalist dad.

I've worked with all sorts of celebrities, from Zoë Kravitz, Jennifer Lawrence and Cara Delevingne to Kate Moss. I once did a Prince video. Salma Hayek was hanging out with him at the time and he asked her to direct the first single from 3121 'Te Amo Corazón'. So we all flew to Morocco, and stayed in then-Italian *Vogue* editor-in-chief Franca Sozzani's hideaway house in Marrakech. I also work a lot with Julianne Moore, and I had a lovely conversation when I worked with Viola Davis from *How to Get Away with Murder*.

I'm actually quite shy, so I've had to get over that, because my work often means I'm in an intimate space with individuals. I've not only got to crack their wall, I've got to persuade them to let me in. I can't put make-up on them if they're going to be difficult with me, so I have to make them like me, and it has to happen quickly. After all these years, when I met Viola I was like, 'Woof, she's a tough nut to crack. She's got some presence, my

God. OK, maybe I'm twittering on too much, I'll just say less, and just gradually, I'm just going to earn her trust.' By the end of it we were having a really incredible conversation about Jim Crow. She has a big soul. People just need to protect themselves, and they have their reasons.

My curiosity about the world and different people's stories definitely comes from my father and the greatest tragedy I carry with me is the fact I'll have to go to my death not ever really knowing it in full. The best way for me to track him is to just go to Trinidad, which should be easy because it's a small country and he was a journalist. I haven't yet been because it's such a massively emotional thing for me, a Pandora's box. It's not hoppity skippity, back to my aunties in Trini for a little holiday on the islands – it could be tragic, it could be beautiful but most likely, it'll be a combination of both. It's something that I want to do, but I have to be psychologically ready. It's my journey and no one else's.

Waiting for the right moment to travel to the Caribbean is the case for many second-generation people who have parents they didn't really get to know. A lot of people just never will: it's not something they want to dig up. But because of the kind of person I am, I feel that I'm more likely to do it. I've always had a desire for information, and a discomfort in not knowing. I think my father died a man that was slightly broken-hearted, and whose dreams weren't realised, and my mother was too unusual for her generation. What I do carry with me is my father's long, delicate fingers, the ones that my mother loved – and I'm so glad for it.

MY FATHER'S HANDS

While researching this piece, I was able to find more details on the passage of Kay's Trinidadian journalist father, Kenneth Luke Montano, who travelled to the UK in 1937, aged nineteen, on a boat called the Cordillera, *alongside his relatives Beryl Montano, aged forty-four, and Barbara Montano, twenty-one.*

NINE NIGHT

Natasha Gordon

as told to Charlie Brinkhurst-Cuff

Natasha Gordon is an actor and writer whose first play, Nine
Night, *explored the death rituals of Jamaicans in the UK.
After smashing the box office at the National Theatre,* Nine
Night *was given a West End run. Gordon has appeared on
TV in* Line of Duty, EastEnders *and* Little Miss Jocelyn.
Stage work includes The Low Road *at the Royal Court,*
Red Velvet *at the Tricycle and* As You Like It *for the RSC.*

I used to think about death a lot as a child. I wondered whether the people in my family would die when they were supposed to, and who would go first.

Caribbean people have death in their roots, in the fabric of their culture and in their connection to the spirit world. We've become so used to abandonment, losing people early and seeing death on a regular basis, that it's become a transitory part of life, rather than being the end. When my mum talks about death, I know she's not talking about the conclusion of her existence.

Nine night is one of the traditional ways Caribbean people celebrate and mourn the death of a loved one: by spending nine nights sharing stories, drinking, dancing, singing and eating together before the spirit, or 'duppy', finally leaves this earth and passes on to a place of peace. It's about helping and upholding the family in their bereavement.

It's morbid, but in that way, I think we are predisposed to prepare ourselves to say goodbye. My mum constantly goes to funerals in Jamaica as a way to pass the time. She doesn't always know the person, but if somebody in the village has died, she invariably goes to their funeral, plans what she's going to wear and what she's going to buy. She has a wardrobe full of black dresses.

LINEAGE OF MORTALITY

Everyone in my family was born in Jamaica and many of them moved over during the Windrush era.

My maternal grandad was the first in my immediate family to come in 1960, by boat. He has dementia now, so his reality is always shifting, but recently he's been reminiscing. He says the journey took three weeks, which was longer than expected because the sea was rough. Every morning they would wake up to a map of where they were and sometimes the ship had moved backwards. Along the way they stopped off at some of the other Caribbean islands and Spain. He made the journey alone but he was coming to meet a cousin.

My mum came by plane. We haven't spoken much about what it was like when she first arrived, but I know that she was interested in hairdressing, so my grandad booked her onto a course. She had very beautiful, shoulder-length, Indian-like hair (which I didn't inherit; I have a glorious curly bush). And while she was on this hairdressing course and experimenting with different products, her hair started to fall out and she began to wear a wig. My grandad came into her bedroom one morning and spotted her without it on and went absolutely ballistic. When they lived in Jamaica, he used to do her hair for her before she went to school in the mornings.

Before my mum was sent for, aged sixteen, she lived with her dad's mum (my great-grandmother) in Jamaica, Portland. She had lived with her mum until she was three or four, and then she was given to my great-grandmother to be looked after. I'm unsure of the details, but the reason why her parents didn't stay together was because one family didn't feel like the other family was good enough for their child. I have met my mum's mother once, and I know that she looks like me. Her story is that she stayed in Portland and never moved away. She had another family of around thirteen children, including one uncle that's the same age as me.

I know more about the other side of my maternal family. My great-grandad used to grow tobacco, and they led an agricultural lifestyle. The family home in Jamaica was built from scratch out of the money they made from tobacco. I haven't been to that house, but I've been to Portland and I get no sense that they were growing up in the yard. I envisage it being on sizeable land, within a very luscious, green area with palm trees. I think they were very close to the sea, not so close that they could see it from the house, but only a mile or so down the road; the sea scent spreading up towards them through the air.

My grandad, the eldest of nine children, was a farmer, a milkman and an entrepreneur – he kept cows and bulls and supplied milk for the local villages in Portland. He made decent money from his trade and was able to look after his parents and siblings. He became almost like a parent figure in terms of supporting the family, and when he came to the UK, he would be constantly working to send money back home. He got his first job within two weeks, and never stopped working until he retired. He worked for the postal service, and then as a chef in an old people's home. He cooked us traditional Caribbean dishes, like saltfish fritters, but he also made a mean apple pie.

Nowadays, my mum spends part of the year in Portland and part of the year in the UK. She does touch base here, as she lived here longer than she did in Jamaica and she's pretty distant from her family that are still there now because they've had all of these years apart.

However, like lots of people, she always had a dream of returning home. She absolutely made sure that she was going to do it before she got to an age when it was too late, because that had been the dream for my grandad and his wife, and they never managed it.

SEPARATE TRAUMA

My dad left the UK to move to Miami when I was about seven. I was heartbroken because I was a real daddy's girl. Even though he and my mum had separated three years before, my older brother and I still saw him quite regularly. The first time I got to see him again was when I flew out to America, aged eleven, in 1987. My brother and I would go out there on alternate summers, and he had gone the year before. It came good in the end, in that every other summer holiday until I was sixteen, I was going to Miami. Most people in my class were going to Butlins.

I was upset with my dad for leaving, but I never voiced it. I was always just so happy to be back with him, and in the fold of his family. I had lots of aunts and uncles out there and we had so much fun. It was hard leaving at the end of each summer, and every time I came back, I would feel blue for a couple of weeks as I acclimatised. In some ways America's not so different, but I would spend hours over there watching the television because I would just be fascinated by the amount of black people on the television and in commercials. Subconsciously, I think it might have pushed me toward acting.

It was my dad's older sister who moved to the UK first and went into nursing. Then he came over as a builder and carpenter by trade. But dad was always clear that he was not stopping in England, it was just transitionary. It was a place to come and work hard, make some money (not that it was ever a fortune), and take that opportunity elsewhere. It was always a passing through point. This is essentially why I think my parents' marriage didn't work out.

My parents met in the Finsbury Park area, in north London, which is where both sets of my grandparents lived. There was a Caribbean community there and I always assumed they met at one of the parties that my grandparents held, or through my dad's sisters, but I've never asked. I know that my dad's parents were pillars of their community who regularly held shebeens. On the weekends you went to the Gordons and there would be a big feast of food, dancing and partying till the early hours of the morning.

SPIRITS

After my dad left, my mum had a boyfriend for a few years but mainly it was just us. We were in Finsbury Park for about a year, then we moved to a council flat in Highbury and Islington and finally we moved to Leytonstone.

Living in England wasn't always easy. I remember my grandad talking once about going to a party in Brixton, and having to walk home to Finsbury Park, where he lived, because no cab would stop for him. It's a two-and-a-half-hour walk. He almost laughed about it, because racist incidents were part and parcel of his life – and he wouldn't even name them as such. When my mum got older she worked in an old people's home and she would get comments from residents about them not wanting to touch her.

My brother is seven years older than me, and I watched his experience going through the education system and marked the moments of 'out-and-out' racism he suffered. The girl child was expected to be at home and help mum to maintain and upkeep the house and cook the chicken, whereas the boy child was the hunter and explorer. They were allowed to be out later at night.

It often meant their experiences with racism were overt in some of their interactions with the schooling system and the police.

I was always aware of my Jamaican-ness at school. I went to school in a really diverse area, so I never felt like the lonely black face in a crowd. We'd share stories of seasoning the chicken on Sunday mornings, and come into school with curry embedded in our nails. We had this shared experience of what it was like to grow up in a Jamaican household as second-generation Caribbean-Brits. But then there were things that were particular to my family that I didn't feel like I could share so regularly.

My mum is very spiritual and the sense of spirits existing amongst us is very real for her. So there were things that she would tell me, or things that she would say that we couldn't do that just seemed odd. I couldn't hang the washing upside-down. She would get so infuriated if a T-shirt was hung the wrong way round with no explanation as to why. It was 'because I say so'. Knives couldn't be placed with the blade facing upwards. The logic was there, in that it could be dangerous, but for her it was just that it invoked some kind of unwanted spirit. I was sceptical, but always sleeping with one eye open, just in case.

FIRST PLAY

I was born in 1975 in Finsbury Park. I wanted to study law until I was about fifteen, but I always loved drama. In my second year of secondary school, we got a new drama teacher, Mrs Henshaw.

She was extremely passionate about her subject and made it clear that her lessons were not an extended break time. You either took it seriously or you left the classroom.

She told me I had a gift for acting and encouraged me to apply for drama school after completing my A Levels. I had been attending the Anna Scher Theatre school in Islington but had no idea that acting was something that you could study full time. My mum, who had her heart set on me becoming a barrister, was mortified when I decided to study at the Guildhall School of Music and Drama, but by the time I graduated I had her full support. Once other people told her I was good, of course, she was very proud. Mrs Henshaw still comes to see everything I'm in. She never tells me in advance but always leaves a note at stage door, full of praise, and instilling in me the same confidence she gave me when I was twelve.

When I left drama school, I was playing the mouthy south Londoner in pretty much everything. Then I got to my mid-twenties, where I no longer looked young enough to play the mouthy south Londoner, but not quite old enough to upgrade to 'mum'. My career had a ten-year lull where I constantly felt a lack of opportunity to keep exploring and practising my craft.

It was then that my friend, Sharon Duncan-Brewster, gathered me and a few actor friends together in a group we call The Brunch. We would meet in the foyer of the Olivier Theatre (in the National at Southbank), and voice our frustrations, share experiences and think about what we wanted to do moving forward. Personally, I discovered that I wanted to write. And not just write – I wanted to articulate something specific: the fascination I've always had with the differences between Caribbean funerals and British ones. So I started to write a few scenes of my play *Nine Night*, until I lost confidence and tucked the script away.

Everything changed when my step-grandma got cancer and passed away in 2014. For the first time, I found myself experiencing what a nine night really was.

My grandma's nine night did go against tradition in one way in that there was no music. My grandad, who was obviously in shock after losing his wife of fifty-odd years, put a padlock around the sound system. Music was central to his core, and he and grandma would have this unspoken agreement, where she would have the television on playing her soaps, and he would just be playing the sound system in the same room, at the same time. It just worked somehow. But when she died his shock manifested itself in such a way that he couldn't play any music for months. And nobody could touch the sound system.

Because there was no music, I remember the voices. There were lots of stories from people I hadn't met before, or people that I hadn't seen for years. I had no idea who most of them were, but they had some idea of who I was. This constant flurry of voices, and the smell of food, the kettle being boiled, the table being full of wine bottles, and Bombay snacks. There was constant movement, but every now and then I would look over to my grandad who would just seem lost. Like he was looking around for her. It was almost like he just didn't see us. He was just searching to find her, within it all.

I decided to start writing and researching the play again with more fervour after the nine night was over. I had found the whole thing an inconvenience initially. People coming around at any time, bringing food, expecting food. It was crazy. Slowly, I learned what it meant to honour a loved one for my mum and the older generation, through researching the play I came to realise what an amazing, cathartic celebration it could be for me too. I had no idea how deeply rooted it was in our West African ancestry. When you get past what the practice is, and dig deeper, you discover that it's a tradition that came over with the slaves, transported to the islands over centuries. They would have observed it in different ways and in secrecy most of the time. It's interesting to ponder how they did it and how much of the tradition we have lost and can't reclaim.

Depending on whereabouts in Jamaica you're from, there are different rituals that you observe. The one that I explored and which features in the play was the Kumina, a ritual of dancing, singing, drumming and possession that makes contact with the dead. It's said to have originated from the Africans who went to Jamaica after emancipation as indentured labourers. In areas like Portland and St Thomas, it's performed at nine nights, births, weddings and christenings.

I've never seen one, but I've been told that they happen sometime after midnight. There has been a huge feast, where the guests have sung songs to celebrate the life of the dead, and there's been a sacrifice, typically a goat. At that point, the duppy chooses somebody to pass through, so that they can relay a message onto the living. There's a female drum and there's a male drum, and they have a rhythmic call-and-response relationship which is key to invoking the spirits.

When I finally finished the first draft of *Nine Night*, in 2016, The Brunch were some of the first to read it. My friend Rakie Ayola, who has played Hermione in *Harry Potter and the Cursed Child*, slammed down the last page, and went, 'Right! That's got to go on, in THIS building!' She said, 'I am serious, you send that to the National Theatre Studio', which is the engine room for new writers. Instead, because I still didn't have the confidence, I sent it off to two director friends, one of whom is an associate at the National, and he sent it on to the studio instead. They asked me to write another draft, and then they called me in for a workshop.

I had completely told myself the story of, 'Well, that was it, I *wrote* a play, I finished it, and some people read it, and some people liked it. Great, I'll get back to my acting job now.' But at each stage people responded to it, and went, 'More, more, more, more, keep going.' And then suddenly, we're here and the play has sold out at the National and is set for a West End run. Although it tells the stories of fictional characters, it is completely reflective of my experiences.

MY NINE NIGHT

Although it's awful that death has such a proximity to Caribbean people's existence, I really think it is more healthy to talk about it. Lots of white, British people that have seen the play have said to me how nine night feels much more conducive to helping you on the road to process death and heal. You never come out in the same place when you experience a seismic loss. It's impossible; death alters you. But there is a way to *be* with it, and it's so important to be able to talk about this thing that has this physical impact on your body, never mind what it's doing to your psyche.

I definitely want a nine night of some kind when I die. I don't want my family to go through all of the consecutive nights, but I would love a day that is separate from my actual funeral which brings together different elements of who I am. The fact that I meditate and the fact that I chant based on Hinduism, means I would love a south Indian priest to be there, alongside the Jamaican hymns, alongside the Kumina drums. I want *all* of that and I have a smile on my face when I think about it.

One thing I haven't done is put it down in my will. I'm yet to sign it, because it's the final seal, isn't it? Whereas at the moment, I'm still able to skirt around it. I need to get on with that.

BARREL CHILDREN

Kimberley McIntosh

as told to Charlie Brinkhurst-Cuff

Kimberley McIntosh is a policy officer at Runnymede Trust, a UK-based race equality thinktank which focuses on research, network building, debate and policy engagement – and who were instrumental in raising the issue of the Windrush scandal to the highest levels of government. She is also a writer, commentator and columnist for outlets such as the Guardian *and* gal-dem.

When I went to Jamaica for the first time aged ten, I saw kids wearing my old clothing. One had on my old Nikes, and another had my old bike. The Nikes were almost tie dye, two different shades of blue with white merging into them. And my bike was baby blue. It was disconcerting.

We were in Lilyfield, a tiny little place in the Parish of St Ann's, near Brown's Town and Bamboo. The village has a shop, church and one main road running through the centre, bordered by houses. What I didn't realise until we got out there was that my grandma was bankrolling the whole village. Since she had moved to the UK in 1960, it had always been her dream to build a house 'back home' in Jamaica, with a big outdoor space. Not only did she achieve that, but she also looked after as many people as she could in the process.

Before she came to the UK, my grandma, Daphne Hill, was a dark-skinned, poor woman working for a rich white family. When the woman she was working for was dying, she gave her the money for the fare to go to England. My grandma took the opportunity, leaving behind her two eldest daughters; my mum's two half-sisters. She was meant to meet her baby father in England, but he didn't show up at the Southampton docks. She waited for a while but then travelled to Reading with another passenger.

She ended up moving to Reading permanently and worked at the Gillette razor factory, and then she worked at the Royal Berkshire Hospital as an auxiliary nurse, which is where Kate Middleton was born – and me, and my mum. It took her ten whole years to save up to send for her eldest children, but she did it. They took a flight over and hated her initially, because they were like, 'Why did you leave us?' and they had actually thought my grandma's sister was their mum. But over time they began to understand the situation.

By the time I knew her, my grandma was well established in the community, very popular at church, outgoing. Everyone used to call her sister. She was skinny and medium height, with short black hair because she never went grey, and sometimes she wore a wig with cornrows under it. Gran was extremely lenient on me as one of the youngest of all my cousins. She would make me peppermint tea from the garden in the morning and let me watch *Barney & Friends*. But she was certainly not someone to suffer fools. I would not mess with her and no one with sense would either.

She didn't tell me a huge amount about her life, so the memories I do have of her are important. We didn't share enough stories about her journey to the UK, and because she's passed away now, those stories are lost. What I do know is that she loved the Queen in that weird, colonial way. And that it was really cold when she arrived. They just had one heater in the house they originally rented in Reading.

Despite this, it's always been obvious that my family has a strong connection to Jamaica, which is why I think my mum, Jackie McIntosh, was so keen for me to go and see what life was like there from a young age. My family normally pick one person that they meet on a trip back home that isn't related to us to support when they come back. Last time they went, for instance, there was someone that was really nice to them and had been talking a bit about their kids' school fees, so they paid them.

'Barrel children', like the ones I saw dressed in my old clothes, and my aunties when they were still living Jamaica, weren't uncommon. Gran would have a barrel at her house in England almost permanently and once we had filled it with our outgrown clothes and other items she would send it to Jamaica. Family members still in Jamaica would distribute the goods so there was little guarantee they gave them to the allocated people. When my aunties were still living in Jamaica, their aunt would give clothes my gran had sent for them to her own children instead.

On that first trip, I remember also being confused that people didn't have shoes or didn't know their shoe sizes, until my mum explained. We once had to draw around a kid's feet onto a piece of paper to take to the shoe shop. After that, I didn't have a problem with my mum sending my old stuff away – apart from this one time when she packed off a pair of shoes that my friends from uni had all pooled together money to buy me. That was annoying.

It wasn't just the poverty. By taking me to Jamaica, my mum also wanted me to see that there were people in positions of power that looked like me. She'd point out policemen or judges (not that judges were just walking around). She impressed upon me that there are places where there are people in every conceivable position that are black, and that is the norm somewhere, even if it's not a norm in the UK. I even spent a day in a Jamaican school, and that was really fun. I was a novelty in the class with my accent and I noticed that I was ahead of the class in maths. They gave me a notebook to work in and we played games in the playground.

My mum's always been really big on aspiration because she grew up really poor. Gran had five kids and she was a single mum, so they didn't have anything. I think my mum always wanted it to be different for me. Taking me to Jamaica built into an expansive plan of making sure I was ahead in life and school. She taught me how to read and write at home when I was very young, surrounded me with role models, and tried to be the best parent she possibly could be – especially after she divorced my dad.

It's her perseverance that led me to university and eventually to my job as a policy officer at the Runnymede Trust, who have been directly involved in elevating the voices of the Windrush generation by working with a coalition of charities like the Joint Council for the Welfare of Immigrants and Praxis in addition to politicians like David Lammy and Guy Hewitt, the Barbados

High Commissioner. Amelia Gentleman's reporting in the *Guardian* put the scandal on my radar in a big way but the country responding to it in the way it did was a bit of a surprise. The stars aligned with public opinion and we were able to organise a media campaign and hold an event in parliament with twenty-five MPs, the immigration minister and powerful testimonies by those affected, such as Sylvester Marshall (alias Albert Thompson) who had been denied cancer treatment, after hospital staff questioned his immigrant status.

On a personal level, I found handling the Windrush scandal very emotional. I was having to do TV interviews while near tears. The whole thing was disgusting and incredibly illuminating in terms of how Theresa May and the Conservative government viewed the Commonwealth. They call it a relationship between nations, but the word 'common' suggests that it's inherently equal. They also call it voluntary, like a group of nations united by a commitment to human rights, which is completely absurd. In reality, the relationship is completely unequal; it's directly inherited from colonialism and the British Empire.

The fact that May didn't have an accurate sense of public opinion and initially wouldn't even meet the Caribbean leaders just shows how disparate the nations are. They're not even seen as important enough to have a discussion with. It's also offensive that the Home Office knew about loads of these cases which had been raised by civil servants and nothing was done. People have lost their homes, livelihoods and their families.

The Windrush scandal affected people who had previously

never questioned their sense of identity – people like my gran who were and are patriots, who love the Queen and thought they belonged here. Whatever people in this country threw at you there was never a question that you were British, and to see that challenged and what it did to them emotionally was heartbreaking. Interestingly, my gran didn't ever trust the state, even though she loved the Queen. She made sure all of her children had their immigration status sorted and always said, 'This isn't going to last. It's easy now, but it's not always going to be easy.' It was like a premonition.

I'm confident that people will get compensation, but how much that will be I don't know, or whether it will be commensurate with the emotional trauma they have been through. They might need to get legal representation because what they're offered is not enough. But I do think for this generation in particular, when they get their citizenship, their cases will be resolved, they'll get their status and they'll be allowed to stay in the country. Whether that's going to be enough to compensate for the loss of home, job and emotional trauma . . . I doubt it.

Sadly, I don't think this is going to lead to a wider criticism of the hostile environment policy put in place by Theresa May when she was Home Secretary. The problems are going to come with the people who've already been deported. It's uncertain what will happen to them. If they had any engagement with the criminal justice system, then in my opinion there's not a chance they'll be allowed to come back to the country.

I do feel a connection to Jamaica when I'm there, but I'm also definitely 'from foreign'. I can understand patois but I wouldn't even try and attempt it because I'd sound like a caricature. It's definitely not my home but it's a place I care a lot about and I've been trying to get a Jamaican passport for a few years now. The bureaucracy is a nightmare but I've got to have a backup because the West is failing!

I was seventeen when my gran passed away and I wish she could see what I've achieved since then. I think she'd be proud of my interest in her country, and our shared history. I didn't really have the same level of interest when she was alive because I was young, in an almost all-white private school. I was trying to move as far away from anything that made me stand out as possible.

I'd love for her to see that what I've chosen to do is to try to make the lives of her descendants better. I wish she could've seen the interest I now have in our culture and the place that she was born and everything she did for us. I think she would be happy.

DEPORT HER

Myrna Simpson

as told to Charlie Brinkhurst-Cuff

Myrna Simpson is the carefully spoken mother of Joy Gardner, who came to the UK from Jamaica in the 1960s. Joy died at her home in London during a violent, botched deportation in 1993. Her case, which has never been resolved by an inquest, shows that the deportations of Windrush-era citizens follow a pattern of hostile immigration policies that stretch back further than 2015. Myrna is still fighting for justice.

They put a leather belt around her
13 feet of tape and bound her
Handcuffs to secure her
And only God knows what else,
She's illegal, so deport her
Said the Empire that brought her
— BENJAMIN ZEPHANIAH[*]

On Wednesday, 28 July 1993, police and immigration officers went to my daughter Joy Gardner's flat in Hornsey, London and broke down the door. They went in and took her out of her bed, where she had been sleeping with her five-and-half-year-old son, Graeme. They took them into the living room and sat on top of Joy, tying her hands with a leather belt at her sides. They strapped her legs and wound 13 feet of surgical tape around her head and face. They put a body-belt around her waist and leg irons on her feet. I think she died there and then by suffocation. That's what the family autopsy said.

---

[*] Zephaniah, Benjamin. "The Death of Joy Gardner". *Propa Propaganda*. Bloodaxe Books, 1996. www.bloodaxebooks.com

When David, my son, came over to my house to tell me that he'd heard from police officers that Joy was in the hospital, I thought that she had met an accident. I was living in Edmonton at the time, and I got dressed quickly to get to Whittington Hospital. I couldn't believe what I saw when I got there. A few police officers milled around, and Labour MP and black activist Bernie Grant, who went on to help lead the campaign to get justice for Joy before he passed away himself in 2000, was there too.

They showed me to Joy's bedside and when I saw her, she had strings and baking foil all over her, and a ventilator pumping air. I said, 'What is the baking foil doing on her?' and then I asked the doctor what was wrong with Joy. Her face had bruises on it. He said to me, 'Mrs Simpson, let me be frank with you, Joy hasn't got a chance.' I was in shock. 'What's wrong?' I asked. 'Is her brain swollen?' He replied, 'Yes, her brain is swollen.' And I said, 'But she's dead, isn't she? She's dead.' He looked very sad but he didn't answer me. I started crying and my children started crying. We were making such a noise in the hospital because I think we had gone crazy. Although we saw her, we couldn't believe that she was gone.

Joy stayed in the hospital for four days. She was rotting in the hospital bed, and they had to spray out the room because of the smell. It was horrible. I slept on the floor for the four nights that she was there because they didn't give me a bed. A church sister of mine came up and stayed with me. I only left to go and have a bath and get something to eat. After four days and nights, we had to turn off the life-support machine because they said that her

227

kidneys and liver had failed. Her death is recorded as 4 August, but in my opinion, her organs had failed from the time she was in the flat. That's where they killed her.

MY TEARS WILL CATCH THEM

I am a part of the Windrush generation. My first vote was in this country, and here is where I made my home and family. I came to Britain when I was only a young woman, in 1961, to pursue a better life for my children and to work. We who are the Windrush generation historically made sacrifices to enable British democracy to flourish. We have earned the right to have a level playing field when it comes to immigration. The hostile attitude that contributed to my daughter's death must be put in the context of the current Windrush scandal.

When I got to England, I didn't sit down; I worked in the snow, frost and fog as a care assistant, washing English people's knickers and cleaning up their messes. I couldn't even get a proper place to live. We used to stay in one room of a house and do almost everything in that room. The landing would be where we cooked. Some people might believe we had life easy, but we bore it rough.

Joy was only seven when she was left with my mother in Jamaica. She was my first child, who I had when I was only young myself, and I didn't enjoy her back then. But I wanted her to stay in the Caribbean until I could provide for her in England. I would send money and visit her every year. When Joy came in 1987 she wasn't illegal, she was legal. I paid 600-odd pounds to bring her to this country. And when I came, sixteen years before, I paid £75 for the aeroplane. She didn't come on a boat or stow away. They maintained that she was illegal because she overstayed her six-month visa. And then they killed her.

We have to try to remember Joy as a student, as a mother, as somebody who was studying media. She grew up in Long Bay, Portland on the sea coast, and every Sunday, without fail, went to church with her grandmother, whether she liked it or not. That was the principle of our Christian family. She moved to Kingston to pursue her dreams but she got pregnant with her eldest daughter, Lisa. She wanted the best for her children and sent Lisa to a private school in Jamaica and had big plans for her future. She was strict and would buy Lisa books instead of toys so that she could start reading at an early age.

Joy went to study at St George's College in Kingston and then she worked at a parish council in Jamaica, where she was given the nickname 'Burkey' (Burke was her maiden name). She left her children with my mother in Jamaica. Joy wanted to be a journalist before her dreams were cut short – similar to the case of Stephen Lawrence, who wanted to be an architect and was killed just two months before Joy's death.

I've received no state assistance in fighting the case whatsoever. Joy's inquest was postponed, and I don't know why they didn't ever reopen it. She was buried without the inquest reopening. When I went to a private barrister about the case, he said that there was nothing that could be done.

I'm sorry for the policemen who I believe killed her. Three of them were tried on manslaughter charges in 1995 and they were all acquitted. But you can't kill someone and get away with it. Even if you get away from man, you cannot get away from God, because there's a true and living God up above and he watches everything that every man, woman and child does. One day, the policemen are going to give account for the loss of Joy's life.

Sometimes I think it will be on their conscience until they die, but other times I think that they cannot have had a conscience, because of the way they treated Joy – another human being. It shouldn't matter the colour of our skin. We didn't choose to be black, they didn't choose to be white. No man should be a racist.

We miss Joy very much and I'm not glad that she's gone from me, but I think she died for a good reason. She hasn't given her life just ordinarily: she's a martyr and she's set examples for others.

I may be old but I'll get justice for Joy. It's not easy when you've lost a loved one. I've tried my best and I'm fighting. I'll fight until I have no breath left in my body because I'm not only fighting for Joy – I'm fighting for everybody, whether black or white, if you have been killed unlawfully. Only God can take the life out of me, no man can take my life.

As of 2018, it's been twenty-five years since Joy was taken away from us in a brutal way. I don't wish it to happen to anyone else. But one day there will be peace in the valley.

THREE LITTLE BIRDS

Corinne Bailey Rae

as told to Charlie Brinkhurst-Cuff

Corinne Bailey Rae is a musician who shot to fame in 2006 with her single 'Put Your Records On'. The soulful singer, whose father was born on the two-island nation of St Kitts and Nevis, was born in 1979 and brought up in Leeds where she still lives, although she spends much of her time touring the world with her husband and daughter.

I was that brown girl that would sit picking the beans out of her rice and peas because I didn't like them.

I felt welcome amongst my Caribbean family and I knew I belonged, but at the same time, I felt my difference. I always had a tender head and never really enjoyed getting my hair plaited or combed because it was so painful. While my little sister was getting all these amazing braids, I never wanted anyone to comb my hair, let alone braid it. My nana would always be like, 'Ah! Ah! You don't brush your hair?' There I was, digging my peas out of the rice, a skinny strip of a girl with none of the Caribbean curves people associate with women from the Islands. Between the fussy eating, my hair, my skinniness, and the fact that I often couldn't understood her accent, I felt like my nana must have slightly despaired of me.

Nana showed her love for me by her actions. She cooked for us every Sunday at my grandparents' beautiful, large house, and me and my younger sisters Candice and Rhea always got matching outfits from her at Christmas. Of course, I now know there are loads of skinny Caribbean women and there had been plenty of skinny kids in my family before me. In my dad's childhood photographs, he and some of his sisters have those legs where the knees are the broadest part!

My dad was born on the tiny two-island nation of St. Kitts and Nevis in the Eastern Caribbean, and he grew up racing lizards and swimming in the sea every day before school. He received a scholarship for a private school and was well educated before being sent for by his parents in England. He had a very close relationship with his grandma and aunties and uncles, all who helped raise him while his parents began to make a life for the family in England. I never hear him speak patois, but he has a lilt to his accent, and he still feels very connected to St Kitts.

In St Kitts, my grandad had worked as something akin to an overseer or a security guard on a sugar plantation. Like so many others, he came over to Leeds in the 1960s as part of the Windrush generation. He prepared a place for the family, and then he sent for his wife, my nana, with the children coming over subsequently in ones and twos. St. Kitts at the time had a close link with England and school children learnt all the English rivers, towns and counties by name. My dad used to read traditional English children's books like Biggles, W. E. Johnson and Billy Bunter by Charles Hamilton, as well as the 'Classics'. His imagined England was all hot buttered muffins by the fire and naughty public schoolboys – a gentile, friendly iteration, captured in the 1920s. The Caribbeans really did think of it as the 'Motherland' and a place where they would be welcome.

At first my grandparents rented, and then they bought a home – but the plan was always to accumulate some wealth and then go back to the Caribbean. As the children got older, they married people from the UK and the whole family ended up staying here for longer than they thought they would. My grandad got a job on the trains with British Rail, while my nana worked in a cosmetics factory. They took a step down coming to England in terms of the sort of work they could get, but it was still more lucrative than being at home, despite the costs of living being higher.

At my grandparents' home in Leeds, Chapeltown, people spoke softly, politely and in that measured style which might be considered more 'English' but it was a familiar way of speaking from the Caribbean. When my grandad would have his cricket friends over, or my cousins would talk amongst themselves, they would sometimes speak patois, or use colloquialisms straight from St Kitts. I would understand it to listen to, but I would never slip into it because it's not from my immediate family culture. I guess I am sometimes aware of being on the outside of that language.

My grandparents' house was a really beautiful, big old thing with swirling brown carpets and a T.V that was permanently on, and in my memory, always muted. It was boiling hot all year round, so we'd race in through the front door and then just strip off to our vests and go play. The hallway had a plastic covering on it to protect the carpet, which made a 'swish, swish' noise when you walked on it. For years, I didn't know they had a typical Caribbean front room, I just knew that that's what *their* room was like. It was always really magical and perfectly clean. They had a black velvet scroll, with the

St. Kitts map on it, a radiogram, a pink sofa with doilies all over the back, and ornaments in a sort of glass cabinet with a mirror. We only really went in that room for Christmas.

The Christmas tree was silver tinsel that you could pack away at the end of the season. We'd open the Christmas presents in there and do a little concert, and I'd always play my violin.

I always felt my Caribbean family were quietly proud of my musical abilities. The violin was an instrument with real status (also played by my three older male cousins) and when I played for them at Christmas, my dad would tell me I was getting better every year. It definitely wasn't a family where you'd *over* praise children. They would come to watch me in concerts, and they might say, 'That was good!' but they wouldn't rhapsodise.

My heritage definitely affected my music, because it's given me an outsider perspective. I was a woman from a working class family who was outside the accepted feminine beauty standards of the time – a black girl who was skinny with afro hair. It made me identify with punk and indie music, to find those individual, expressive voices who were and shaking things up. I delved into African American music as I saw it as the poetic expression of black excellence that I had been searching for. It shows in the graceful pioneers – like Duke Ellington, Jimi Hendrix, Stevie Wonder, or Miles Davis.

I enjoy playing festivals in the Caribbean, but I'm definitely seen as a little bit of an anomaly. I embrace that because I'm never going to be this voluptuous Caribbean woman with braids down my back, speaking patois or singing reggae. I do feel like there's a part of me that doesn't feel 'authentically' Caribbean, because

I've been brought up in the UK and because my mum is white. I've always felt open to being teased in that world.

The literary side of Caribbean culture has been a big 'way in' for me in terms of exploring my identity, and the more I explored the multi-faceted nature of Caribbean expression and the further I moved from a surface, stereotyped reading, the more I felt at home with my Caribbean-ness. Caribbean voices, like Linton Kwesi-Johnson, burrow into post colonialism, Caribbean identity and how it engages with Britishness. My dad represents that reality as well; in that he is a deep-thinking introvert – a computer guy who is interested in maths. He was my first example of blackness. He has an elegance that I know to be Caribbean, though it flies in the face of the image of the Caribbean man as the 'jovial party person' that we are still fed in wider culture.

TALKING TO WHITE PEOPLE

My mum made it her work to raise us in black culture. She met my dad when she was 17 and they got married when she was 19. She fit well into my dad's family and went out dancing to Blues clubs with him and his sisters when they first got together in Leeds. We went to Carnival every year (Leeds West Indian Carnival is the oldest in Europe), and deconstructed everything we saw on T.V. I studied English Literature at Leeds University, and both my mum and I have read all Toni Morrison's and Alice Walker's novels, as well as masses of black literature; it is one of our favourite shared pastimes to discuss this work. Mum read Reni Eddo-Lodge's *Why I'm No Longer Talking to White People About Race* before me which, if you know her, is typical! I think it's brilliant. It's your duty to culturally engage if you have a child who has a different ethnicity to you and it's always been really great to have a parent who knows that. She's what people might call an 'ally'.

If I had had a racist experience at school, I would more likely have gone to my mum and said 'This thing happened' or 'This person called me that', and we would talk through it. She felt more approachable because I didn't want to burden or sadden my dad, I wanted to insulate him from it.

Obviously I learnt more about my blackness in a soulful and direct way from just being around my dad, and his way of existing. There's a very dignified aura to my family, which I really associate with the Caribbean. He was certainly brought up around col-ourism and pigmentocracy, but St. Kitts was, nevertheless, a *black majority* culture. The policeman was black, the judge was black and the teachers were black. The bank tellers, and the shopkeepers, and the green grocer reflected him. Even though when my family came to England they faced prejudice, I don't think it was deeply internalised by them because they always had the Caribbean to refer to as place of black independence.

My family never explicitly talked, around me, about facing racism in the UK and I feel like it was their deliberate intention. Moving to England, they wanted to present greater opportunities for their children, and grandchildren, to flourish, grow, succeed and have a good education and get good work. I remember when

I did my spellings once with my dad, and one of the words was 'prejudice'. I asked, 'What's prejudice?' and he said, 'Prejudice? Well imagine if you were Chinese, and then you were somewhere and the people don't like Chinese people and they just judged you because you were Chinese.' He went out of his way to give me an example of racism that wasn't about being black.

RETURN TO ST KITTS

The first time I went to St. Kitts was when I was on honeymoon with my husband (after being widowed in 2008, I got married again in 2013). We were supposed to be staying in Antigua, but I looked across the water and saw St. Kitts on the horizon and I felt this unassailable impulse to go.

We got on a plane which took about twenty minutes and went to stay with my Nana, who has built a big house there, and moved back when I was 16 or 17. It was incredible to see her house, as I remember her building it from the UK. For many years I didn't realise that all the time she was working here she was saving for a house. Once when we went to her home in Leeds, she was unwrapping a huge package at the dinner table. It was a sample of a large terracotta floor tile for her new front room 'back home'. That's the first time I realised what she was building.

On arrival at St. Kitts, my great uncle picked me up from the airport. I hadn't seen him since I was a child. My auntie said to me that I'd recognise him because he looks like an older version of my father, and as soon as he walked in, that's exactly what I thought – he was an older, smaller version of my dad; my dad in the future, like in a time machine.

He drove us round the island, and pointed out the house where my dad grew up and the place where they would run out of the house in the morning and go and swim in the water, just like taking a bath. At that exact moment there were little boys just running and diving into the water. It was really easy for me to imagine my dad's childhood. It was idyllic, semi-rural: waking-up, going swimming, quickly getting ready for school. Playing football for an hour on the school field before school started. Running home for lunch, because it was all so near. Playing sport after school, and then swimming in the evenings.

The safety of growing up in a really small community where you knew all the adults must have been so reassuring. There were hardly any cars and he had a lot of freedom, even as a five or six-year-old, although in school discipline reigned and he had to go to church three times on a Sunday. It must have been a big adjustment coming to England, even just in terms of weather. When they came they didn't have any coats – and it was snowing. When my aunt first saw their terraced houses, she thought they were moving into a factory.

When I went back to St. Kitts, I was able to put my family in a new context – the place that had nurtured and shaped them. Here was the sunshine, here was the garden. My nana had a small garden in England, but to see her amongst the flowers, pointing

239

out the different things she'd grown, her roses, guava and mangoes, was special. We were trying to keep the green 'vervet' monkeys off the trees because they are my nana's nemesis. 'The monkey eat up the mango', is what she's always saying.

It felt like St Kitts was her natural environment. That pace of life, where you sit on the veranda and you say a few words to someone, then there's a pause, and they say a few words to you. You talk, you ask questions, you look at some photographs. She had a photo of me from my first album and I felt really proud that she had this picture, way over there in the Caribbean where I wasn't sure my music would have reached. She also had all these old photos of when she got married, wearing spotless white gloves and intricate lace. She's still so lovely looking now, but my grandmother was insanely beautiful when she was a young person. I'm always looking at photos of this woman with these high cheekbones and beautiful eyes and a very easy femininity and imagining her life.

For her to be back in the Caribbean must feel like a circle completed. She's able to enjoy the fruits of her and my grandfather's labour. I admire how they lived so frugally in the UK in order to build a house in St. Kitts where they could sit and enjoy the view and the space. My work takes me all over the world, but unlike them, I've never made a huge decision to pack up everything and to start out anew, not knowing what life would hold. I admire that bravery. As my parents met and married in the UK my life story wouldn't have happened without nana and grandad deciding to start a new life in a new country.

FLOUR AND WATER
INTO BRICKS AND MORTAR

Riaz Phillips

Riaz Phillips is the author of Belly Full, *a series of books aiming to promote African and Caribbean food, culture and history across the world. The Oxford graduate was inspired by the opportunity to bring elements of his upbringing to a wider audience by his Jamaican family. He founded publishing company Tezeta Press in 2016.*

Caribbean food has a special aura about it. The level of excitement it inspires in people, be it at a funeral, christening or birthday, is unrivalled. It's hard to pinpoint why this is, but the complex ethnicity of the Caribbean certainly plays its part. Influences from Europe, Asia and Africa mean that there's a taste and texture profile that can appeal in any given meal, while the colonial legacy of many of the foods being used to give plantation workers strength for the day shines through.

My primary introduction to this legacy of food was through my father's Jamaican mother, Mavis Bucchan. Born Mavis Henry in 1939, she migrated to the UK on a large cruise ship a few years after the eminent *Windrush*. Though she was in her mid-teens when she moved, she never completely lost her Jamaican accent, nor her recollection of her home in the south-eastern Jamaican parish of St Catherine's. With my paternal grandfather hailing from the much smaller island of St Vincent, my other grandfather moving to the USA years before I was born, and my parents both being born in London, my grandmother Mavis was my link to Jamaica and Caribbean food.

Following her passing in 2017, my interest in Caribbean food and culture as a whole blossomed. I had spent the past few years dedicated to documenting Caribbean food in the UK through my book, *Belly Full*, and her death, alongside the countless stories I heard from Caribbeans reminiscing about the tropics, made me decide it was time to visit Jamaica in early 2018.

I hadn't been to the country in almost a decade and, fearing for my safety, my family in the UK and America made attempts to deter me from going. They feared I might be caught up in the throes of crime and violence that are frequently broadcast on the news. However, after years of seeing people with no Jamaican heritage visiting and having the time of their lives, the calling was impossible to ignore. When yet another snowstorm was on the horizon in London, I hopped on a plane with four days' notice for a solo three-month excursion.

Jamaica immediately felt like home. Entering a food establishment thousands of miles away usually requires some form of hand-holding, but the menu boards I saw in Jamaica read like a meal in one of my family's kitchens. From birth, I had been indoctrinated into the ways of Caribbean cuisine and my immersion in Jamaica was immediate.

Spending most of my time in the hills away from Western news I was quite removed from life back home. The only thing that gave away my alien status was my thick English accent and, upon hearing it, people kept asking me if I was a deportee. As I tuned in to life back home, I soon came to understand why: the early months of that year saw the Caribbean community as a whole come to the forefront of the international media as it emerged that many who came over during the Windrush era were being deported due to the hostile environment created by the Conservative government. I thought it was common knowledge that Caribbeans supported the health and transport industries post-war so it was a shock to realise just how many people in the UK were unaware of their plight and the context behind the deportations.

My family, like many others, were assured of a better life with more opportunities in the UK, which turned out to be untrue. Now, after decades of being naturalised and contributing to the economic and social landscape, their peers were being threatened with deportation. I always recall the elders telling us of the strife they had 'coming over on boats' and leaving their family behind. 'We didn't know how easy we had it,' they would say. Even with all the hardship they went through there was always a hint of nostalgia in their stories which usually centred on music and food.

BLACK AND WHITE

With few public places accepting patronage from black people, the atmosphere of Kingston, Jamaica was recreated in basements and houses across the UK, from west London to south Manchester.

Parties centred on the pulsating ska rhythms of the day, and

– accompanied by rice and peas, curried meats, fried dumplings and rum – ran deep into the early hours of the morning. The popularity of these parties bubbled from the underground and eventually moved to the streets, as carnivals in London, Leeds and Bristol emerged as a response to racist maltreatment. With makeshift steel barrel jerk drums, and Caribbean kitchens creating Trinidadian rotis out of the back of vans for revellers, arguably the street food phenomenon we see today saw some of its early foundations at these carnivals.

Records suggest that early instances of Caribbean food and drink establishments, i.e. cafés, bars and social clubs selling Caribbean food and cooked meals, date back to the late 1920s, with the founding of the Caribbean Café at 185a Bute Road in Tiger Bay, Cardiff and Florence Mills' Social Parlour in 1929 at 50 Carnaby Street in central London (founded by Sam Manning and Amy Ashwood – a political activist who was the first wife of Marcus Garvey). It was described as an intellectual hub where 'guests were attracted to the rice 'n' peas West Indian cuisine". But apart from these outlets in some of the main cities in the UK, foods from 'back home' were said to be 'mostly still a rarity on these shores'.

For the new immigrants in the 1960s workplace, assimilating to English food proved a problem, too. In an interview conducted with Caribbean migrants in Manchester, a Ms Edith Stanley,

---

* Grant, Colin. *Negro with a Hat: The Rise and Fall of Marcus Garvey.* Oxford University Press, 2008, p.437

who travelled to the UK on the *Windrush* voyage, recalls: 'The canteen food was horrible. West Indians are fussy over their food. We used to take a food flask to work.' As supermarkets and local grocers primarily served British produce, 'shops did not offer the exotic foods of the islands: dasheens and yams, soursop and mango, salt fish and black-eyed peas.' As Edith tells her interviewer, 'You could not get rice; the only rice was for making rice pudding.'

As times progressed, scores of enterprising individuals were able to combine what tropical produce they could find and mix it with European foodstuffs to create the basis of sustainable businesses that were not only able to provide jobs for their communities but also spaces of gathering for displaced people.

The first notable wave of eat-in Caribbean-owned establishments came in the late 1960s as youths of the Windrush generation era started to come of age. Places such as Frank Crichlow's now-closed Mangrove Restaurant on All Saints Road in Notting Hill, west London, Roy Shirley and the Johnson family's R & JJ West Indian in Hackney, east London, Dougie's Hideaway Club and West Indian Restaurant in north London, and the infamous Black and White Café in Bristol's St Paul's, all opened within a few years' timespan. In other places across Britain, eateries opened by the first generation of immigrants have become part of local folklore in lieu of documentation.

While these places often competed with youth centres, bookmakers and bars as places of Caribbean congregation, the disintegration of these other spaces over the years means that today food eateries are amongst the last vestiges of our community. Arguments about which shop has the best patties or curry goat mirror tiffs over which aunty or uncle cooks the tastier version of a certain meal. What strongly linked these places – from the butchers, bakers, cafés, or dance functions – is in the fact that they represented public spaces free from persecution. They were places to see familiar faces who were going through the same distresses, a place to ask 'Wagwan!', to not have to feign an English accent, to touch fists, or to gossip about anything from bereavements to infidelities back home.

SUNRISE BAKERY

A spontaneous trip up to Birmingham's outer region of Smethwick helped shine some light on this. Between the 1940s and late 1960s, owing to the expense and prolonged shipping times of importing many foodstuffs across the Atlantic Ocean, there was scarce access to Caribbean cuisine of the variety that we are familiar with today. Many turned to what they could recreate with readily available items.

Sunrise Bakery, formed officially in 1966 by Jamaica transplant Herman Drummond and his business partner William Lamont, is one of the oldest and now largest Caribbean food institutions still in operation in the UK. With a smaller Caribbean migrant pool than the capital in London, the black community in the Midlands of England appeared more tight-knit and the pair quickly became known faces. With this wide social network cast, Drummond and Lamont began to sense a level of malaise that many new migrants had in the UK and came to understand the food stuffs they missed the most.

Using basic ingredients and a well of experience from working in the baking industry back home, the pair were able to recreate Drummond's family's recipe for hard dough (hardo) bread, bulla cake and spiced fruit bun in the UK. Selling them via a self-delivery service around the area and travelling to other people's houses, commerce for their baked goods grew.

Errol Drummond, Herman's son, who operates the now industrial-size business, told me stories of how his father faced difficulties in getting the business off the ground, including gaining access from local landlords for somewhere non-residential to run the food production. Eventually they settled for what they could find and afford, which was a garage in Birmingham's northern region of Edgbaston. They began primarily by selling the baked goods within the city but soon found themselves expanding across the Midlands to places like Wolverhampton and the Black Country – Dudley, Walsall, Sandwell – where other Caribbean and African communities had grown.

Thanks to the growing number of Caribbean grocery stores, takeaways, clubs and shebeens, word about Drummond's business soon spread beyond Birmingham's predominantly black areas. After Errol took the reins of the business, he started targeting London; first he sold in corner shops and then, aiming high by winning contracts with a number of national supermarkets, the business exploded. This immediately called for an upscale in space, which resulted in the move to the factory locale where Errol now heads the business.

Errol recalls how his father left Jamaica with an ambition to build a better life for himself, and to send for family back home. While he undoubtedly achieved this goal, Errol still alludes to the difficulties he has as a Caribbean-centered business and the void of understanding that surrounds Caribbean culture.

When I recounted this story to younger business owners while on my travels around the country, they weren't nearly as surprised by it as I was, as the same things were still happening to them today. Difficulties getting leases and unhelpful landlords were part and parcel of being a black business. For then to struggle all those years and still face the same issues as their grandparents really elucidated how despite progress, there is still so much more to be done. However, not being completely pessimistic, it also illustrated the power of food as a commerce that could circumvent even the harshest discrimination and racism.

DINNER AT HOME

In my grandmother's one-floor flat in Hackney, east London, I'd eat an array of meals in the type of room immortalised by writer and artist Michael McMillan's *The Front Room*, which has come to typify Caribbean migrants. It was a vivid attempt at emulating the well-to-do British class in what was allegedly the

Caribbeans' mother country. Dinners here, perched upon floral placemats, were eaten facing a wooden dial television and a glass cabinet containing china plates, silver teapots and cutlery we never touched. When I look back to most of the twenty-six years I essentially lived there, I don't ever recall them being taken out and I'm not sure they ever did in the decades before – when the same flat housed my father and his three siblings.

My half-siblings, friends from the area and I would look at the tableware in awe and wouldn't dare think about touching them or 'ramping' about near them. Indoor tennis and football was relegated to the home's long corridor, with its patterned carpet that resembled the fabric on London Underground seats which connected the bedrooms.

The desolate day my grandmother passed away, the whole family congregated at the flat. As we solemnly rummaged around, I realised that it wasn't the objects themselves that had any particular significance, but rather it was her presence amongst them and her reverence toward them that made them so special. As I, for probably the first time ever, sifted through the silver trim plates in the cabinet, I found that I actually had far more regard and nostalgia for the regular blue floral plates that were kept in the kitchen. I'd gone off to university outside London, sandwiched with long trips abroad, and my drowsy summer stays had dissipated to just a few hours or so when I was back in London. Though I think I'd dropped, broken and secretly discarded a fair few of those floral plates over the years, a number remained, and as soon as I touched them I immediately recalled years of dishes she had made, like stews, oxtail, saltfish and 'hard food'.

Between the tables of my grandmother and numerous aunties, these dishes were so common to me as a child that I had assumed it was what everyone ate. It wasn't until I started going round to friends from different backgrounds – white, African, Turkish, Asian and everything in between that you find in north-east London – that I realised the food we had was different. On Sundays, roast potatoes and sprouts were mixed with yams, green bananas and a wealth of other produce that would draw blank stares when I mentioned them in the playground.

I never asked where this food came from originally, or why my grandmother religiously made weekly pilgrimages to Dalston's diverse Ridley Road Market for them. Here, come rain or shine, she would spend time feeling and sifting her fingers through piles of island produce. As a child I didn't quite understand why she was so determined to make this journey when she could have just gone to the supermarkets half way between to buy what all the other people in the area ate – like pizza, chips, turkey drumsticks and burgers.

I think subconsciously watching my grandmother carry out this routine over years, even when her leg eventually slowly succumbed to a debilitating disease, hammered home to me just how important this food was to her. Like many others in my family, she had a desire to carry on the same culinary traditions as those before her and I could see the pride that was involved in the process. On the rare occasions I would go on these excursions with her, the guaranteed run-ins with at least two other 'aunties' (which had me thinking every black person in Hackney was my cousin) making the same laborious journeys and engaging in the exact same process shone light on just how important this practice was to so many other people.

Even with all this, I still didn't understand fully. Why the journeys? Why the special untouched plates? Why the dedication to making these particular meals that nobody outside our community ate? It wasn't until the day my grandmother passed away that it hit me I'd never have an opportunity again to ask her directly about her early days in the UK. This is when I started my adventure across the UK meeting the people and families behind the oldest and most renowned Caribbean food institutions in the country. I think I tried to vicariously have those conversations I never had with her through the many wonderful people who have given their lives to the continuation and promotion of Caribbean food and culture in the UK.

Through hundreds of conversations, one key theme appeared to come up over and over again: the opportunity food can provide. Whether it was trying to impress other immigrant families or trying to appear well-to-do for white people, food and a good meal played a key part in social bonding and elevation. Food has allowed immigrants not just to survive, but also to prosper. I was able to piece together parts of my background that I never fully understood through the frank, direct conversations I had with my interviewees. They were more willing to have straight conversations with me than my protective family members.

THE POWER OF FOOD

Caribbean identity may be a drop in the ocean of black identity, but for black people in the UK, diaspora culture sees people clinging to the past for pieces of their identity. Caribbean, and most noticeably Jamaican, food has emerged as the predominant food of black Britain and played a large part in changing the food landscape. We brought a wealth of tropical produce – from herbs and spices like pimento and hot peppers to the ubiquitous jerk – to this shore and in the process popularised them and introduced them to a larger audience. It has added to what was once a bland food scene – consisting of pastries, native vegetables and meats devoid of seasoning. Now 'jerk dressed pork', 'coconut sponge cakes', and 'vegetable curry' find themselves in the most popular of great British cookbooks (see Jamie Oliver – but don't try his 'punchy jerk rice').

The older generation always saw the power of this food, which is why they were so determined to have the next generation learn how to cook it. My grandmother probably would have imparted a lot more food wisdom onto me if I wasn't so fixated on playing video games, but that seems to be the way the tide is turning for Caribbean food in the UK. As time removes British Caribbeans further away from their roots and the original familial and religious structures, fewer and fewer are carrying on these culinary practices.

This isn't just an issue at home – many legendary Caribbean

food stops like Harlesden's Mister Patty, which closed in 2012 after forty years of business, are in danger of fading away as nobody else in the family wants to go through the same strife to maintain the business. It's fortunate that a small wave of new eateries such as Buster Mantis, Rudie's and Ayannas are pairing their Jamaican heritage with an in-depth knowledge of the UK food scene to keep the culture flourishing.

The legacy of the Windrush generation runs deep in the realms of healthcare, education and even travel. For those within the community it's clear to see how Caribbean food has provided the basis of rebuilding neglected parts of the UK and, in the process, lighting the fire of street parties and street food (both ironically now turned into multi-million pound industries) seen today. Praise and adulation seems apt, rather than deportation.

Lack of knowledge about the Windrush generation seems to mirror lack of knowledge about Caribbean food, but through food I think we can keep this history alive. It's important that all descendants of Caribbeans can see the opportunity I saw travelling across different communities across the UK. We turned flour and water into bricks and mortar and changed the world.

YOU ARE JAMAICAN

Jamz Supernova

as told to Charlie Brinkhurst-Cuff

Jamz Supernova (Jamilla Walters) is a DJ who blends rap, bass, house and alternative R&B to make her own unique sound. She attended the BRIT School before joining Radio 1Xtra, where she now holds down a regular future R&B show. Three of her grandparents are from the Caribbean and her father was affected by the Windrush scandal.

My maternal grandad Orlando Mcdonald was a reggae artist who took the Swinging Sixties by storm. He was almost like a rock star, with lots of women on his arm. He had moved to the UK from Jamaica when he was sixteen to join his mum because he'd apparently got someone pregnant. He used to own a restaurant in Birmingham called Xaymaca, the original Arawak name for Jamaica, meaning 'land of wood and water'. You had to do the limbo from the bar to enter the restaurant itself, where they served dishes like curry goat, ackee and salt fish, and rum and ginger cakes.

My Irish nan used to get a lot of stares, living with her three mixed-race children in Tamworth, a market town near Birmingham. There were only three other black families in the area. After she passed away from ovarian cancer when I was ten, my grandad said that she was 'the only woman I've ever loved'. I thought, 'Well, you should have treated her a bit better then.' He would come and go and I don't think they ever lived together.

I remember our family all being at Xaymaca one summer night and he had his two exes and former partner there. Strangely, they all got on well.

My grandad wasn't always around but he still encouraged my mum to be proud of who she was. 'You're black, you're Jamaican,' he would tell her. 'You need to work twice as hard.' He was so upset when she got pregnant at eighteen that he didn't talk to her for a while.

On my dad's side, my grandma is from Cuba and my grandad is from Jamaica. Both of my parents were born in the UK, but that hasn't stopped my dad from facing difficulties with the Home Office. In 2015, the same year Home Secretary Theresa May enacted the hostile immigration policy, we went to renew my dad's passport so he could take my sister on holiday to France. They asked him to come in for an interview and said, 'We can't prove who you are.' Since then, the way he has been treated is despicable.

In his teenage years, my dad had started using the name Roger James 'Sewell' rather than his given name, Roger James 'Walters', to appease his father. Later in life, he then legally changed his name to the Africanised 'Tunde Oba', to rid himself of the slave surnames so many Caribbean people carry. But the lawyers made a mistake with the paperwork and legally changed his name to Tunde Oba from Roger James 'Sewell', not 'Walters'. This gave the Home Office the ammunition they needed to claim that he wasn't who he said he was, and so start a long process of passport rejections, despite my dad providing them with ample evidence.

It became more than about him not being able to go on holiday, which he can't, but about the security which he no longer has. They asked him, 'Why did you change your name to an African name when you're not African?' You have to wonder if they would ask 'Tom' why he changed his name to 'Rob'. He said they treated him like a criminal but I think they chose the wrong person. He can fight it if he wants and take it to court, but not everyone has the means to do so. I think they purposefully chose to do it to people they think are stupid or poor.

The situation didn't make me feel less British, but it made me angry because my dad is British and he was born here. In some ways, I think I'm angrier than he is because I view it as an outright disrespect to treat someone in the way he's been treated. It raises the question, who is really British? And if we go around accusing people, where does it end? Lots of people in this country have family members who are immigrants.

CARIBBEAN OR AFRICAN?

I spent my formative years living in New Cross, in south-east London. I went to quite a posh primary school, and then a diverse school called Deptford Green for secondary, which was a culture shock. I remember thinking it was weird because all my friends got into those posh secondary schools even though I was smarter than them. It was distressing, but now I know how they pick their intake, and it's not just about smartness, it's often to do with race and class.

For the first two years at Deptford Green, all I did was play football. There was a really dominant female group that ran our year and I kept my head down because I didn't want to be noticed or get into anything. Even so, I'm glad I went there because it was incredibly multicultural. You'd have African, Caribbean, Vietnamese, Somali, Turkish and white British kids all together. The whole class was a rainbow, with no culture dominating. I feel like I've been around so many cultures, going to friends' houses, learning their languages. I fancied every single type of boy that you could have imagined.

However, I didn't think about my Caribbean heritage for a long time. I was a little bit embarrassed, possibly because I didn't spend much time with my dad's side of the family or my maternal grandad, who were all from the islands. In secondary school, it became more confusing because you were either Caribbean or African, but alongside changing his name, my dad changed mine and my brother's last names to Oba too. All through school people would say I was lying about being from the Caribbean and would joke that I was from Central Africa.

Before I started working at 1Xtra, I actively didn't like Jamaican dancehall music, but by working on different shows, I quickly became fascinated by how much music came from there. When dubstep was happening, I was able to link all the dots. It's so interesting that this one little country has created this whole branch of music.

Like many British underground music genres such as jungle, drum'n'bass and grime, dubstep was strongly influenced by Jamaican sound system culture. Dub music in particular was one of the early musical art forms to come out of the Caribbean. Dubstep, like dub music, puts production emphasis on the beat and the drums alongside sparse instrumentals. There have been seminal records that have bridged the gap between dub and dubstep such as Skrillex and Damian Marley's 'Make It Bun Dem' and 'Breakage' ft Newham Generals and David Rodigan.

Music is in the blood of Jamaican people, and almost everybody knows an instrument. It could be from slavery, when music was surely used as a form of release and resilience. Going to Jamaica for the first time with work allowed me to embrace the culture and meet lots of different people. It took seeing it through their eyes to really appreciate it. It can mess you up, not knowing where you're from, and finally, I felt this sense of 'I'm fucking from here!' Before then, I had never really thought about being black. Afterwards, I realised I wanted to know myself deeper and took an Ancestry DNA test. We have to remember that no one is from Jamaica genetically because of slavery and colonialism.

Despite his name change, my dad is muted about his identity and blackness nowadays, and I wonder if it's because he's already worked through his identity issues, rather than him being part of the second generation of Windrush children who, from the outside, seem to care less than the third generation does. My mum told me that growing up, my dad was always searching existentially.

They met in drama school, where they were both training to become actors. When she got pregnant, she carried on studying and worked as a drama teacher while having me and my brother in short succession. I don't know how she managed it, with two kids under the age of three. My dad was acting himself, so he wasn't always around.

They broke up when I was three or four years old, but I remember it being a creative household. As my brother and I were so close in age, we would do elaborate role-playing games. He would be the judge even though he was a baby. My dad liked to draw, and I remember doing that with him a lot. While my mum has continued to express her creative side through writing, my dad stopped acting when I was ten and got a normal job.

BRINGING JAMZ TO THE BBC

I always loved music. My radio show focuses on forward-thinking, alternative R&B and I dabble in electronica and jazz music. The music I DJ in clubs is multi-genre with an underlying UK bass focus. I grew up listening to traditional R&B, like Ashanti and TLC, but started raving to funky and tribal music.

I wanted to be a singer when I was younger, but I couldn't really sing. Thankfully, my mum told me I was great at other things

261

and to park it. When I went with a friend to the opening of the BRIT School (a college for performing arts and technology) and saw the radio studio, that was it. I left Deptford Green behind and entered the world of radio. I love editing and the creative side of it, bringing something to life. When you're on the air, lonely people often get in touch with you to talk, which is something you can't get from a playlist.

I felt really wanted at BRIT. It opened me up because I was probably the least kooky person there. Every other day someone was coming out as gay or coming to school in pyjamas, and no one cared. We were able to challenge each other. I remember there was a girl in my class whose dad went to Thailand and came back with a wife. I think I made a joke about it and it really upset her. It forced me to learn about social cues. Keep it in your head, man, or don't think it at all.

I finished BRIT with a BTEC, decided I wasn't going to university and started interning at 1Xtra instead, with the aim of becoming a presenter. For five years I kept doing pilots and the feedback was 'you're not good enough'. Sometimes it would leave me in tears, but I kept going because I was so passionate.

When I was working there, I also had my own show on Reprezent, a community radio station in Brixton. I soaked everything I was learning at the BBC in and applied it there. What those five years taught me was how to deal with rejection and jealousy. Because when I finally got my show on 1Xtra, I didn't care any more – even though I was overwhelmed with how proud people were. I was the first young person from community radio whose trajectory people could emulate.

The things that make you different and stand out are what you bring to institutions like the BBC. I'm bringing something they don't have and maybe have never had before. Culturally, despite how it sometimes feels, we are needed. From a business perspective it's not rocket science; with more diversity, you make more money and reach different audiences. My radio brand and what I represent comes from my identity and my Irish and Caribbean heritage. It comes from the fact that my black experience might be different to someone else's black experience.

More than thanking my grandparents of the Windrush generation, I'd like to thank my parents, who dedicated their whole lives to getting us out of the situation they grew up in. They were so adamant that we would never live the life they lived, with the lack of money, that I've always had food in my fridge, clothes on my back. I've never really wanted for anything. Having that security as a child gives you a different mindset. One that lets you succeed.

Even so, I think it's important to explore your history, where you're from and be proud of it. We're not homogeneous, and when people say, 'Oh, you're not really black' for one reason or another? Fuck all that.

INVISIBLE PASSENGERS

Maria del Pilar Kaladeen

Maria del Pilar Kaladeen is an academic specialising in the history of the system of indenture in the Caribbean. She left school at fifteen and returned to education as a mature student. She is one of the editors of We Mark Your Memory, *the first international anthology on the system of indenture. Her monograph,* With Eyes of Wonder: Colonial Writing on Indentured Indians in British Guiana, *is forthcoming with Liverpool University Press.*

It was the summer of 2008. I had not seen Ronald for ten years. I had not seen him since I escaped to university and became the only one of the five of us to get a degree. I had been running away, acquiring bits of paper to prove I was not like my older brothers. In the time since I last saw him, Ronald had been sectioned at least once and imprisoned multiple times for petty crime. He had been in rehab and out of rehab. This is what the paperwork of his life would show. Me? I had acquired a BA, an MA and a teaching qualification. I was also two years into a PhD. I was still running. But on that day in the summer of 2008 I had acquired a piece of paper that I didn't expect. It was our eldest brother David's death certificate. I had to stop running. I had to go to Weston-super-Mare. I had to find Ronald. I had to tell him that after years of sleeping rough in London, Babylon had finally killed him. David was dead.

If it wasn't so sad I'd say it was rich with metaphor, this story of how the great-grandchildren of those rendered homeless by

Empire and defined by their lack of a nation ended up literally homeless and walking the streets. In British Guiana (now Guyana), where our ancestors came from India to work on the sugar plantations, they needed a pass to leave the estates to which they were indentured. To be found without one would mean being charged with vagrancy. Their lives lost meaning to the coloniser if they weren't involved in the industry of Empire. For if we weren't making sugar, what purpose did we serve?

In the final decades of the indenture system, 'free' Indians, those who had completed their periods of indenture, were harassed by the police if they were found homeless in the nation's capital. People spoke of 'sending them back'. Some voluntarily went to the immigration depot hoping to return to an India that they had not seen for perhaps a decade or more. It is not a coincidence that V. S. Naipaul's *A House for Mr Biswas*, the story of a man's quest to own a home, is widely considered to be *the* novel of the Indian-Caribbean experience.

Three of us identified the body: my dad, my youngest brother and I. We registered the death and then went to the undertaker opposite the hospital. I cannot remember at what point we agreed it should be me – that I would leave London the next day and find Ronald – that I should be the one to tell him. I do remember understanding why it should be me. Telling Ronald would have been one of the hardest things on the death to-do list. He and David had been close when they were young. They shared a room and guarded each other's secrets for nearly a decade. I was also tough enough to tell him because I was the youngest and least close to David. I had been indifferent to him for much of my life, this guy who had spent most of his time in his room and who I remembered as moody and sardonic; who had to die for me to realise how much I loved him.

I think about the last time I saw David. I was coming home from the British Library, walking towards Euston Station. There's a large grassy space in front of the bus stops and restaurants that mark the entrance to the station. In summer you see people lying on the grass. From the fence that separates the grass from the street I saw a man talking to a tree. I kept walking. I saw a can of lager at his feet. I kept walking. I saw him pointing to the tree, remonstrating with it, accusing it. That man is mad, I thought. And then, at some point, after having walked two metres or so, I realised I knew him. 'Oh fuck,' I thought, 'that's David.'

It turns out that membership of the British Library does not save you from your past or uncomfortable present. I wanted to drop the transparent bag that held my research, and which was compulsory in the reading rooms. I wanted to run towards him and shake him back into the world, but I was terrified. I watched him from further away for five minutes as he continued his discourse with the tree. Eventually I walked away.

Two years later I come home late from something or other with my husband. As soon as we walk through the door the phone rings. My dad is on the phone, agitated; he tells me he's been calling my landline all day. I laugh, 'Why didn't you just call me on my mobile?' As I finish asking, it occurs to me that it must have been something he could not tell me until I was safely home. And just like that, he says that David is dead.

I love my brothers. You would need to be of our west London-Indian-Guyanese-Spanish tribe to understand how I feel about them. You would need to know the song that we made up about the glow in the paraffin heater and you would need to have sat with us in the early morning, before we left for school, as our cassette player whirred through a tape-to-tape copy of *Thriller*. You would need to share the psychological bruises of the vicious white hate that smacks cricket bats over your 'Paki' head and calls your parents 'fucking foreigners'. You would have needed to be there the night the dog shit hit the window and, because it was the seventies, listened while nobody explained to you why. You would have needed to stand in your night-clothes, outside your bedroom and listened to your parents speak in shamed tones to the police about whichever one of us had been nicked this time.

I set out from Paddington to find Ronald not really expecting success. At some point in the journey I discovered that a fire had broken out on the pier in Weston-super-Mare early that same morning. I could still see the smoke as I walked away from the station and towards the town. It added to the strangeness of the day. My dad had given me his last address; he seemed confident that I could find him there. But when I knocked on the door a young guy told me he no longer lived there and seemed reluctant to give me more information. I understood immediately. It emerged that he had been kicked out of the house, one of the many rehab spaces in Weston-super-Mare, for drinking and taking drugs. I want to say that he fell off the wagon but that sounds like something mildly glamorous that happened to male Hollywood stars of the 1950s. It is not a term for the dejected like us, particularly when it emerges that since he was kicked out, Ronald has been sleeping in a public toilet. The guy tells me that he loves Ronald, that the two of them had become great mates while sharing the house, but that he must keep away from him or he won't be able to stay sober. He tells me that if I walk around town, I might just be lucky and run into him.

I understand this young guy completely. Ronald was a hurricane who blighted my childhood. He began drinking when I was a little girl and he was a teenager. He would come crashing through the front door and into inevitable pained confrontations with parents for whom his behaviour was unfathomable. He felt guilty about the trouble he had caused for years after. One night, when my youngest brother and I were small, we tried to drag him up the stairs so that he wouldn't be discovered in a stupor and we wouldn't be kept awake by shouting. It was fruitless. He was a giant to us then. I told him this story once when he had been sober for about a year. He did not remember it and he felt terrible that we had been involved. I was never angry with him because I had never believed that he had a choice. When he was sober he was a different man. He was charming, funny, kind and streetwise. He was the dual-heritage Artful Dodger.

I must have been there for a few hours. I walked by the sea, stopped for coffee, wandered in and out of shops. Then, eventually, possibly when I was close to giving up, possibly after I had called my dad to tell him that I had no luck and would be heading home soon, I saw him walking towards me from the seafront. From far away he looked tanned and healthy and it was not until he got closer that I could tell he was totally off his head. I can't explain to you the look he gave me. As though he was asking himself, 'Am I dreaming? Is she there?'

It all comes out so quickly.

'Do you remember me?' I ask.

'Of course I do,' he says, stunned.

I can see he's trying to form the words to ask me what's wrong, but he's fighting through chemicals to be with me in a moment that he knows holds something terrible. I tell him to come with me to sit on the wall by the beach. I tell him that I have bad news and just like that he says, 'It's David, isn't it? He's dead?'

I wondered how he knew and it's only now I realise that he must have lost others to the streets. Intermittently homeless since he was a teenager, he would have known better than I that the average age of a rough sleeper at death was around forty-three. David was exactly that age when he died.

For some reason we ended up leaving the wall and walking around town. We kept running into people he knew. It was almost comic. I was half holding him up as he cried and then he would transform as he greeted an acquaintance and whisper to me: 'They send all the old criminals from London here now. It's like a reunion – we all know each other.' I left him within a couple of hours. He did not come to the funeral and we did not hear from him for months and then one day my parents received a postcard in his handwriting. It simply said: 'I am broken-hearted about David.'

BROKEN BY THE SYSTEM

The majority of Indians chose to stay in Guyana after completing their period of indenture. Of those who stayed, many were savvy enough to realise that the only thing that could safeguard their children from the sugar plantation was education. In colonial Guyana this meant British schools and British literature and British history and British every-damn-thing. Even before the turn of the twentieth century, Guyana had its first professionals of Indian-Guyanese heritage. Thus the colonial structure that tied you to the plantation was also, perversely, the means by which you could escape.

Education is how we became British enough to think of England as home, to emigrate as part of the Windrush generation. Yet we were invisible to people here who knew nothing of Guyana, never mind the story of indenture. The white elite that write the majority of our history books and create our syllabuses have chosen to remember the abolition of slavery as the story of British colonial plantations in the Caribbean of the nineteenth century. Nobody lingers on the fact that after abolition, a system was created to replace enslaved labour and that its worst facets were to use coercion and dishonesty to uproot hundreds of thousands of Indians and deliver them like parcels to the waiting whips of overseers on the plantations of the Caribbean, South Africa, Mauritius and Fiji.

There is a narrative of the Windrush generation that emphasises their success, their compassion, their tenacity and capacity to give. Even in the face of ugly hatred and baseless contempt they wrote novels, joined the armed forces, became bus conductors and tube drivers, delivered babies, taught children, wiped arses in hospitals, served food, entered the civil service, went to university and even joined the police force. Many don't like to complain; the most you will get is an admission that they had to 'endure' or 'put up' with discrimination in the workplace, overt racism and violence on the streets. Our narratives of success, of superhuman achievement, of parents who passed university exams while working all hours and parenting are true, but only promoting these narratives of our success means we occlude the stories of those that slipped through the cracks, thereby denying the experiences of the victims and the culpability of the institutions.

Ronald and David, born in the sixties, did not stand a fucking chance in retrospect. Their school was so bad it closed down shortly after they left. I remember watching from the bus as the kids who went there threw each other into the artificial pond outside Charing Cross Hospital. My dual-heritage brothers were an anomaly in that school where almost all of the kids were from white working-class backgrounds. Ties knotted in a half-arsed way, shirts out of their trousers, thirteen-year-old chain-smokers who would, a matter of three or four years later, be doing the same jobs as their parents for piss-poor pay. It was a mark of their wisdom that most of them knew this and did not expect more. To them, school was an obstacle to surmount before getting a job.

For young men of colour in this period, victims of institutional racism, there were different obstacles. Yet to say this is to suggest that they needed to be in institutions to be victims and this was far from the case. Every black and brown boy knew another for whom a police stop had ended in an attempted 'fit-up'. You had to be creative to survive or you could be slowly driven mad by it all. By the caretaker who addressed you as 'Half-Jack' instead of using your name, or the elderly white cockney ladies who 'affectionately' called you 'Abdul'. From the life-threatening to the petty, all of these acts combined to tell young men of colour, like my brothers, that their lives had no value. What was most sinister was that as far as the police and courts were concerned there was a clear and consistent message to black and brown men: we can do anything to you and nobody will care.

When my husband came home after I'd returned from my day in Weston-super-Mare I was standing in the shower, shocked and exhausted. I was thinking if I stayed there long enough I would be able to wash it all away. The joy of seeing Ronald and the despair at his situation; the fear of what would happen to him now I had left him alone with this awful news. I asked him to take my clothes and put them in the washing machine. I told him where Ronald had been sleeping and that he had kept hugging me. 'Just wash everything, please. Please just wash everything.'

David does not have a gravestone and no plaque marks the

dates of his life and death. His ashes were scattered in the rose bushes of a west London crematorium because, short of any other place to call home, this is our gaff. He is one of many children of Windrush who were broken by the system. While his name will not be listed in the defiant roll-call of 'successes', who triumphed in the face of adversity, he will be remembered by the people who loved him and to whom he was never invisible.

YOUR ANCESTOR'S WILDEST DREAM

Sharmaine Lovegrove

as told to Charlie Brinkhurst-Cuff

Sharmaine Lovegrove is one of the first black female publishers in the UK. She owned a bookstore in Berlin, before starting her own imprint, Dialogue Books, as part of Little, Brown in 2018. Sharmaine has permanently disrupted the publishing industry.

I have never been afraid of whiteness. As a young woman, I was fiery and I would use my literacy to have conversations and arguments with older white men in their sixties. I spent so much of my life reading that I wasn't afraid to take them on.

The first book I read that connected me to my Caribbean heritage and my blackness was probably *Anansi the Spider*, a Ghanaian folklore character who appeared in stories brought to Jamaica by slaves. I was a precocious reader and, from a very early age, I had a deep understanding of the connection between Jamaica and Africa. I also went to black Saturday schools, set up to counteract the underachievement of Caribbean children in the 1960s, where I learned more about our culture and studied maths and English.

All four of my grandparents moved to England from Jamaica, and they each had a unique journey. My maternal grandfather disembarked at Portsmouth, disoriented, and almost got on a coach to Manchester. We ended up in London because someone ran up to him and grabbed him, asking if he could take his place because he really needed to get up north. The idea of these self-motivating people, able to pick up their lives in one country, move to another, and then have absolutely no control over their circumstances when they got here fascinates me.

Out of the four, I am closest to my maternal grandmother, who came over in 1960. She met my grandad through friends in London, and they started dating. What was unusual was that my grandad is descended from the indigenous Arawak 'Indians' and Jamaican Maroons, who escaped from slavery and created free communities in the Jamaican mountains. It was uncommon for someone so light-skinned and middle class like my grandmother to be with someone so clearly black and from a working-class family. But she fell in love with him, and they moved to Balham in south London and had three children.

My grandad was a very quiet, inexpressive man and eventually they divorced. Like a lot of women of her generation, my grandmother's happiness was not her foremost concern. She worked really hard, had two jobs, and she mainly brought the children up by herself. She's a matriarch, but she holds a quietness within her that tells something of her sacrifice. She would never complain. I don't think people understand the silence within our culture.

My mum had me when she was only eighteen, and it's my grandma who I remember as my nurturer. She was the first person to hold me; she cut my cord and the very first words I ever heard were 'I love you' from my grandma in her strong Jamaican accent. I lived with her until I was six and my upbringing felt very Jamaican. I remember being planted between her legs while she did my hair, standing on a stool to help her make doughy dumplings for the beef stew every Saturday, making sure to keep quiet and out of her adult conversations but always listening. She would wash my face, clean my nose and ears with cotton buds, and when I had a cough, splash white rum on her hands, warm them in front of the electric heater and rub my chest. I am such a child of that Jamaican woman.

Being brought up by my grandmother complicates my third-generation experience because even though my accent and the way I behaved as a child meant I was always having the authenticity of my blackness and my Jamaican-ness questioned, I feel like I'm very much a product of a conservative Jamaican middle-class family. I'm fully myself at all times, but I'm also mindful and respectful.

Even though my dad was the 'archetypal' black Caribbean man, a real rude boy who loved women, music and cars and always had multiple girlfriends, there are people hidden within my family who buck that trend – uncles like Len Garrison, the co-founder of the Black Cultural Archives and a righteous and committed man. My paternal grandfather was also an absolutely incredible man. Standing at 6 foot 3, he had an air of wisdom about him, and he was honest and caring. There are men out there who have worked hard, raised their children right and who have been strong and stable role models. Those men are not really celebrated within our culture. We need to move away from the idea that black men will always treat you in a certain way. It's a myth.

THE LONELY LONDONER

The reason why I have achieved so much in my life is because I have been through so much, but I have never been prepared to stay, be hurt and not be heard. I have always known how to use my voice.

I moved into my mum's house when I was six, and by the time I was thirteen I had started reading books by black women like Toni Morrison and Maya Angelou, which I found on my parents' shelves. *The Color Purple* by Alice Walker was one of the most profound things I'd ever read about black love and pain, meanwhile *How Stella Got Her Groove Back* by Terry McMillan celebrated black women's friendships. It was Jamaica Kincaid's work that got me thinking about the harshness of Jamaican life, the sexual objectification of women and the way in which our voices are gagged.

Sadly, living back with my mother and stepfather in our Victorian villa near Battersea Park, I didn't feel as though I was being heard at all. My mother and I are just fundamentally different people and we had a volatile relationship. So instead of suffering any longer, I did something really courageous and left home at age-sixteen. They were at work when I packed my bags. I didn't think it would be for ever, more that I just needed a break, but when they found out what I had done, they made it clear I was no longer welcome. Through my reading I knew that everyone has to find their own path ultimately; I just didn't think I would have to find it so soon.

I was very influenced by the journeys that my grandparents had taken and the journeys I had read about of people travelling into the unknown. In Sam Selvon's *The Lonely Londoners*, a novel which depicts the experiences of some of the first Windrush migrants, there is a moment where Galahad realises that he is completely alone in the big city. 'He forget all the brave words he was talking to Moses, and he realise that here he is, in London, and he ain't have money or work or place to sleep or any friend or anything, and he standing up here by the tube station watching people, and everybody look so busy he frighten to ask questions from any of them.'*

My experience was not as lonely as Galahad's, so in some ways, it didn't feel so big. *Small Island*, by Andrea Levy, was also a very important book for me around this time because it helped me to understand the loneliness and fear my grandparents would have felt, all the things that they would never have told me about. *The Lonely Londoners* is not a multiple-character piece in the way that *Small Island* is. This is a book about community, how people come together or they don't. Those random acts of generosity and kindness that could completely change the heartbreaking daily grind our grandparents had to go through.

After leaving home, I started off at my friend's house in Balham and then moved around. I was homeless for a year; I stayed in

* Selvon, Sam, *The Lonely Londoners*, Penguin Modern Classics, 1956, p. 23

hostels and even slept rough. My RP accent precluded me from getting the housing I needed as councils and housing associations believed I should just go home. When I was eighteen I moved to Hackney and was living in a warehouse. It was the nineties and I was heavily involved with the Shoreditch and Soho gay scenes. It felt so liberating, and there was a lot of sex and drugs, but I knew not to get completely lost in it because I had a responsibility to myself and my grandmother. I didn't really have any demons because I'd already been through one of the worst things that could happen to someone – being rejected by your parents.

Literature felt like the greatest gift because I always had people in my life who had been through tough experiences: like Margaret, from *Are You There God? It's Me, Margaret* by Judy Blume, or the horrific treatments of the prisoners in Tahar Ben Jelloun's epic novella *This Blinding Absence of Light*. I could never feel sorry for myself when I had them.

Even though I lost my parents, I also always had the unconditional love of my grandma. I saw her independently of them and I spoke to her every day on the phone, and still do to this day. In terms of my living situation, I just knew that the generational gap would mean I couldn't live with her again. At one point I was renting a flat in Balham with some debutantes, and my grandma lived opposite. We didn't have any curtains, and when I'd pop round to see her, she'd ask things like, 'Sharmaine, how many boys are you gon' have at the house?' I'd be like, 'They're not for me, grandma, so don't worry about it.' I was seeing women at this time, not men.

NIGHT WOMEN

I didn't have any contact with my parents for the whole of my twenties. I saw my dad again, once, when I was thirty-two but I haven't seen or spoken to my mother since. During this time, I still went to school and did my A levels, which is a very complicated thing to do when you're homeless, and then I went to university when I was twenty-one. I thought I wanted to make documentaries and so I started working as a runner and as a production assistant, but I was always working in bookshops part-time and for a while I sold secondhand books underneath Waterloo Bridge.

I had started at Foyles when I was eighteen, and by the end of my time there, I was running the black literature section. When they asked me to look after it, I didn't realise it would change my life. It's how I came across authors like Bernardine Evaristo, a writer who transcends poetry and prose; Hanif Kureishi, who captured the working-class, urban London experience of living on estates, perhaps of being in a gang and coerced into a certain lifestyle. That was something I didn't have direct access to because I was considered too posh and alternative, with my Doc Martens, patchwork skirts and unbrushed hair. Working at Foyles also opened my eyes to the fact that there were some alternative narratives that were still missing.

Following Foyles, I worked for Waterstones and the London Review Bookshop, and briefly became a press officer, but I always wanted to have a bookshop of my own. When I was twenty-six and living in Hackney I went to the bank to ask for a loan to start one in London Fields. The bank turned me down and said there would never be a bookshop in such a bad area. Now there are three. But in the meantime, I decided to go to Berlin, where the prices of books were the same as in London, and where they had a net book agreement so that Amazon wasn't dominant. That was alluring because I knew that if I failed it was because of me, not just because of the prices of the books.

So in 2009 I got on a plane and made the second big journey of my life. I loved Berlin. There are a lot of similarities between Germans and Jamaicans. We are incredibly righteous and proud. While Englishness is passive-aggressive, Jamaicans and Germans are more upfront and direct. While in Germany I met the man who would later become my husband, and his father gave me some money to start buying my first books from a wholesaler. I opened my English-language bookshop, Dialogue Books, six months later. It felt like a massive achievement – putting the books on the shelves. I still remember some of the individual customers and the books they chose. It was a very magical and special experience.

SMALL ISLANDS

I left Berlin to come back to London in 2014, ready to explore more of my heritage. One of the books that stays with me from that period is Marlon James's *The Book of Night Women*. It explored the narrative of the slave trade from a Caribbean perspective. His book is the reason that I can't watch *12 Years a Slave* or any other slave narrative films, because I feel like I saw too much in his work. It reminded me that while it's easy for everyone to talk about black women as being matriarchs, rendering them that way doesn't always give them a face, a personality or an identity. Marlon showed that you could be a matriarch in myriad ways.

In May 2016, aged thirty-five, I went to Jamaica for the first time. I've travelled all over, been to every parish and all the major towns and villages, as well as the small places. I learned that it is one of the most diverse countries in the world. I have the spectrum of culture within my family and I've always understood that out of many, there is one people. To be part of the Caribbean is to know that your family have endured so much physically and mentally at the hands of other human beings, for no other reason than the colour of their skin. You can't help but build a sense of pride that your bloodline is a bloodline that survived, fought and kept going.

I'm really pleased I got to go to Jamaica as an adult, when I was already a mother and a wife, and when I already understood myself. If I'd gone when I was younger I'd have got in so much trouble. I'd have been distracted by the sun, the beauty of our people and rippling beach bodies. Instead, I went there with a purpose of understanding my culture, and what I got was something I had always had to fight for in the UK: acceptance. To the people who live there, I was just the child of Jamaicans.

My grandmother grew up with the notion of Britain and Empire, and I love her stories from when she came over, barely twenty-one. While it was challenging, she used it as a learning experience. Britain has really always been her mother country, and it has looked after her. It's where she feels safe. She doesn't have a romantic vision of Jamaica, but she does still have a romantic notion of England.

It broke my heart that the Windrush generation went through the scandal the same year as the seventieth-anniversary celebration. I felt that they were so robbed and that it was a missed opportunity. We're not immune from this happening again.

As far as I'm concerned, the worst thing that I could do – to quote Ava DuVernay – is to not 'become your ancestor's wildest dream[s]'. If there's anything I understand, being from an immigrant family, it's that you do better. I know that I'm going to make my grandparents proud and make everything that they and their parents went through worthwhile, so when I go back to Jamaica and stand at my great-grandparents' graves and pay homage, I can say, 'I did it.' That's how I was brought up. That's what my grandmother instilled in me.

Acknowledgements

Firstly, the biggest thank you to the Windrush generation and their descendants.

Thank you to my brilliant agent Emma Paterson, researcher and photographer Shannei Brown, and last minute reader Megha Mohan (and the Intersectionistas). To editor Fiona Crosby for the commission and her calm editing skills, Sean Costello and Lindsay Davies for their precise copyediting, Jill Cole for proofreading, and everyone else at Headline who has lent their support to the project.

This book wouldn't have been possible without Hannah Lowe, Maria del Pilar Kaladeen, Sharon Frazer-Carroll, Riaz Phillips and Kemi Alemoru – who poured their hearts onto the page for the chapters they have written.

The interviewees who graciously gave me or family members their time were Kay Montano, Rikki Beadle-Blair, Kimberley Mcintosh, Howard Gardner, Natasha Gordon, Paul Reid, Lazare Sylvestre, Lenny Henry, Corinne Bailey Rae, Jamz Supernova,

ACKNOWLEDGEMENTS

Myrna Simpson, Naomi Oppenheim, Nellie Brown, Sharmaine Lovegrove, Catherine Ross, Gail Lewis, Neil Kinlock, Kwame Kwei-Armah, Mark Brantley, Shankea Stewart, Kuba Shand-Baptiste, Everine Shand, Lorna Holder, Cheryl Pearce, Liv Little, Valerie Mcintosh, Joyce Barrett, Heather Barrett, Ella Wilks-Harper, Islyn Wilks, Stephen Bourne, Beverley Davis and Jo Stanley.

Finally, I would like to say thank you to my best friends and colleagues Liv Little and Kemi Alemoru for their endless support, alongside that of the rest of the *gal-dem* editors and contributors, who are incredibly special. My immediate family, Aunty Pauline Cuff, my mum Jacqui Cuff and dad Timothy Brinkhurst have done more than they could ever know to uplift and enlighten me.